Pray

CULTIVATING A PASSIONATE PRACTICE OF PRAYER

SHELBY TURNER

Study Suggestions

We believe that the Bible is true, trustworthy, and timeless and that it is vitally important for all believers. These study suggestions are intended to help you more effectively study Scripture as you seek to know and love God through His Word.

SUGGESTED STUDY TOOLS

- A Bible

- A double-spaced, printed copy of the Scripture passages that this study covers. You can use a website like *www.biblegateway.com* to copy the text of a passage and print out a double-spaced copy to be able to mark on easily

- A journal to write notes or prayers

- Pens, colored pencils, and highlighters

- A dictionary to look up unfamiliar words

HOW TO USE THIS STUDY

Begin your study time in prayer. Ask God to reveal Himself to you, to help you understand what you are reading, and to transform you with His Word (Psalm 119:18).

Before you read what is written in each day of the study itself, read the assigned passages of Scripture for that day. Use your double-spaced copy to circle, underline, highlight, draw arrows, and mark in any way you would like to help you dig deeper as you work through a passage.

Read the daily written content provided for the current study day.

Answer the questions that appear at the end of each study day.

HOW TO STUDY THE BIBLE

The inductive method provides tools for deeper and more intentional Bible study. To study the Bible inductively, work through the steps below after reading background information on the book.

1

OBSERVATION & COMPREHENSION
Key question: What does the text say?

After reading the daily Scripture in its entirety at least once, begin working with smaller portions of the Scripture. Read a passage of Scripture repetitively, and then mark the following items in the text:

- Key or repeated words and ideas
- Key themes
- Transition words (Ex: therefore, but, because, if/then, likewise, etc.)
- Lists
- Comparisons & Contrasts
- Commands
- Unfamiliar words (look these up in a dictionary)
- Questions you have about the text

2

INTERPRETATION
Key question: What does the text mean?

Once you have annotated the text, work through the following steps to help you interpret its meaning:

- Read the passage in other versions for a better understanding of the text.
- Read cross-references to help interpret Scripture with Scripture.
- Paraphrase or summarize the passage to check for understanding.
- Identify how the text reflects the metanarrative of Scripture, which is the story of creation, fall, redemption, and restoration.
- Read trustworthy commentaries if you need further insight into the meaning of the passage.

3 APPLICATION
Key Question: How should the truth of this passage change me?

Bible study is not merely an intellectual pursuit. The truths about God, ourselves, and the gospel that we discover in Scripture should produce transformation in our hearts and lives. Answer the following questions as you consider what you have learned in your study:

- What attributes of God's character are revealed in the passage?

    Consider places where the text directly states the character of God, as well as how His character is revealed through His words and actions.

- What do I learn about myself in light of who God is?

    Consider how you fall short of God's character, how the text reveals your sin nature, and what it says about your new identity in Christ.

- How should this truth change me?

    A passage of Scripture may contain direct commands telling us what to do or warnings about sins to avoid in order to help us grow in holiness. Other times our application flows out of seeing ourselves in light of God's character. As we pray and reflect on how God is calling us to change in light of His Word, we should be asking questions like, "How should I pray for God to change my heart?" and "What practical steps can I take toward cultivating habits of holiness?"

THE ATTRIBUTES OF GOD

ETERNAL
God has no beginning and no end. He always was, always is, and always will be.

HAB. 1:12 / REV. 1:8 / IS. 41:4

FAITHFUL
God is incapable of anything but fidelity. He is loyally devoted to His plan and purpose.

2 TIM. 2:13 / DEUT. 7:9
HEB. 10:23

GOOD
God is pure; there is no defilement in Him. He is unable to sin, and all He does is good.

GEN. 1:31 / PS. 34:8 / PS. 107:1

GRACIOUS
God is kind, giving us gifts and benefits we do not deserve.

2 KINGS 13:23 / PS. 145:8
IS. 30:18

HOLY
God is undefiled and unable to be in the presence of defilement. He is sacred and set-apart.

REV. 4:8 / LEV. 19:2 / HAB. 1:13

INCOMPREHENSIBLE & TRANSCENDENT
God is high above and beyond human understanding. He is unable to be fully known.

PS. 145:3 / IS. 55:8-9
ROM. 11:33-36

IMMUTABLE
God does not change. He is the same yesterday, today, and tomorrow.

1 SAM. 15:29 / ROM. 11:29
JAMES 1:17

INFINITE
God is limitless. He exhibits all of His attributes perfectly and boundlessly.

ROM. 11:33-36 / IS. 40:28
PS. 147:5

JEALOUS
God is desirous of receiving the praise and affection He rightly deserves.

EX. 20:5 / DEUT. 4:23-24
JOSH. 24:19

JUST
God governs in perfect justice. He acts in accordance with justice. In Him, there is no wrongdoing or dishonesty.

IS. 61:8 / DEUT. 32:4 / PS. 146:7-9

LOVING
God is eternally, enduringly, steadfastly loving and affectionate. He does not forsake or betray His covenant love.

JN. 3:16 / EPH. 2:4-5 / 1 JN. 4:16

MERCIFUL

God is compassionate, withholding from us the wrath that we deserve.

TITUS 3:5 / PS. 25:10
LAM. 3:22-23

OMNIPOTENT

God is all-powerful; His strength is unlimited.

MAT. 19:26 / JOB 42:1-2
JER. 32:27

OMNIPRESENT

God is everywhere; His presence is near and permeating.

PROV. 15:3 / PS. 139:7-10
JER. 23:23-24

OMNISCIENT

God is all-knowing; there is nothing unknown to Him.

PS. 147:4 / I JN. 3:20
HEB. 4:13

PATIENT

God is long-suffering and enduring. He gives ample opportunity for people to turn toward Him.

ROM. 2:4 / 2 PET. 3:9 / PS. 86:15

SELF-EXISTENT

God was not created but exists by His power alone.

PS. 90:1-2 / JN. 1:4 / JN. 5:26

SELF-SUFFICIENT

God has no needs and depends on nothing, but everything depends on God.

IS. 40:28-31 / ACTS 17:24-25
PHIL. 4:19

SOVEREIGN

God governs over all things; He is in complete control.

COL. 1:17 / PS. 24:1-2
1 CHRON. 29:11-12

TRUTHFUL

God is our measurement of what is fact. By Him are we able to discern true and false.

JN. 3:33 / ROM. 1:25 / JN. 14:6

WISE

God is infinitely knowledgeable and is judicious with His knowledge.

IS. 46:9-10 / IS. 55:9 / PROV. 3:19

WRATHFUL

God stands in opposition to all that is evil. He enacts judgment according to His holiness, righteousness, and justice.

PS. 69:24 / JN. 3:36 / ROM. 1:18

METANARRATIVE OF SCRIPTURE

Creation

In the beginning, God created the universe. He made the world and everything in it. He created humans in His own image to be His representatives on the earth.

Fall

The first humans, Adam and Eve, disobeyed God by eating from the fruit of the Tree of Knowledge of Good and Evil. Their disobedience impacted the whole world. The punishment for sin is death, and because of Adam's original sin, all humans are sinful and condemned to death.

Redemption

God sent His Son to become a human and redeem His people. Jesus Christ lived a sinless life but died on the cross to pay the penalty for sin. He resurrected from the dead and ascended into heaven. All who put their faith in Jesus are saved from death and freely receive the gift of eternal life.

Restoration

One day, Jesus Christ will return again and restore all that sin destroyed. He will usher in a new heaven and new earth where all who trust in Him will live eternally with glorified bodies in the presence of God.

"Prayer is a place to tip our full hearts over and let them spill out to God's listening ear."

WEEK 1: PRAYER FOUNDATIONS — 13
- Day 1 — *Pray Like Jesus* — 15
- Day 2 — *What is Prayer?* — 21
- Day 3 — *How Should I Pray?* — 27
- Day 4 — *Do My Prayers Matter?* — 33
- Day 5 — *The Ways God Answers Prayer* — 39
- Day 6 — *Scripture Memory* — 45
- Day 7 — *Weekly Reflection* — 46
- Extra — *Aggie Hurst's Story* — 48

WEEK 2: GOING DEEPER: BUILDING ON PRAYER FOUNDATIONS — 51
- Day 1 — *Have Faith and Don't Doubt* — 53
- Day 2 — *Prayer and the Holy Spirit* — 59
  - *+ The Trinity* — 64
- Day 3 — *Praying for Wants and Needs* — 67
- Day 4 — *Praying for People You Love* — 73
- Day 5 — *Prayers of Adoration* — 79
- Day 6 — *Scripture Memory* — 85
- Day 7 — *Weekly Reflection* — 86
- Extra — *George Muller's Story* — 88

In This Study

WEEK 3: PRAYING THROUGH THE HARD STUFF — 91

Day 1	*Praying Through Anxiety*	93
Day 2	*Praying Through Anger*	99
Day 3	*Praying When You Have Messed Up*	105
	+ The Prayer for Salvation	110
Day 4	*Praying Through Sorrow*	113
Day 5	*The Open Invitation to Pray Again*	119
Day 6	*Scripture Memory*	125
Day 7	*Weekly Reflection*	126
Extra	*Susanna Wesley's Story*	128

WEEK 4: MAKING PRAYER A PRACTICE — 131

Day 1	*Praying Scripture*	133
Day 2	*The Place of Prayer*	139
Day 3	*The Time to Pray*	145
Day 4	*Praying in Community*	151
Day 5	*Praying When You Don't Feel Like It*	157
Day 6	*Scripture Memory*	163
Day 7	*Weekly Reflection*	164
Extra	*Lottie Diggs Moon's Story*	166

WEEK 5: MAKING PRAYER A PASSION — 169

Day 1	*The Birthplace of Passion*	171
Day 2	*Praying for the Impossible*	177
Day 3	*Jesus's Prayer for You*	183
Day 4	*Persistent Prayer*	189
Day 5	*Scripture's Final Prayer*	195
Day 6	*Scripture Memory*	201
Day 7	*Weekly Reflection*	202
Extra	*Martin Luther's Prayer*	205

IN CLOSING

What's Next	206
Additional Resources for Prayer	207
In Everything Prayer Journal	208
What is the Gospel?	210

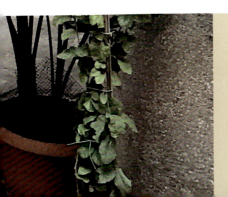

— WEEK ONE —

PRAYER
foundations

Prayer is hard. Harder than it seems it should be.

We are busy, distracted, and unsure if our time spent in prayer is actually amounting to anything.

We want to have a vibrant, passionate prayer life, but instead we have one that is often cold and apathetic.

What is the cure for this? It is a true, biblical understanding of prayer. If prayer is not our passion or priority, it is only because we do not yet understand it rightly.

This week, we will construct a solid theological foundation of prayer on which we will build for the rest of the study. Together, we will study prayer as God designed it and apply biblical truths about prayer to our lives. And then, the lackluster life of prayer we once knew will grow (slowly but consistently, for it takes time) into one that is purposeful, meaningful, and powerful!

Jesus's life is marked by the practice of prayer.

WEEK ONE

day 1

Pray Like Jesus

READ LUKE 5:16, MATTHEW 26:36, MARK 1:12, JOHN 6:15

That long and nagging to-do list. The phone that begs you for your attention each time it illuminates with a new notification. The way all your worries and fears surface when you finally quiet your soul for a moment. The doubt that your small words could matter to a vastly infinite God. These are some of the many hindrances we experience in our prayer lives. If prayer is sometimes hard, confusing, or passionless to you, you are not alone. But you should also know that your prayer life was meant to be so much more than boring and burdensome.

Prayer is meant to be an intimate conversation with God where your requests are welcome, your praise can flow freely, and forgiveness is offered for your every confession. And not only is prayer intimate, but it is also effective. It is a means through which God sovereignly accomplishes His will in you and the world. How do we know that God intends for prayer to be a driving force of our relationship with Him and used to accomplish His will in the world? Because Jesus models this for us.

Jesus's life is marked by the practice of prayer. He prays publicly, privately, in anguish, in celebration, for Himself, and for others. To put it simply, Jesus prays about all things and at all times. If there is anyone's example of prayer that should be followed, it is Jesus's. Today, let's look at three ways Jesus prays that will set the stage for communing with God in prayer during this study. We will examine how Jesus continuously prays with intention and on mission, even now.

One of the most striking ways Jesus practices prayer is in intentional solitude. Throughout the Gospels, we see Jesus withdrawing from daily life and clamoring crowds to commune alone with God.

If Jesus, who is Himself God, purposefully removed Himself from the hustle and bustle to speak with His Father, then how much more do we need to do the same? Maybe the fleeting, half-focused prayers we offer throughout our day are just the beginning of what a thriving prayer life looks like. Maybe if we followed the example of Jesus and set aside intentional alone time to pray and meet with God, we would begin to discover the passionate life of prayer we have been desiring.

We also learn from Jesus's example that prayer is more than just communion between God and ourselves. God moves in response to prayer to do meaningful work in us and missional work in the world (1 John 5:14). Prayer changes things. And specifically, *your* prayers change things.

Jesus prayed for God's will to be done through His obedience in Gethsemane. He prayed for children, healed the sick, and cast out demons through prayer. In the high priestly prayer—which we will discuss in more depth in week five—He prayed for all believers throughout all time to be one with the Father through Him (John 17:20-26). Jesus exchanged innumerable words with His Father and the Holy Spirit as they partnered to bring about the will of God on earth.

When we follow Jesus's example and ask God to bless, heal, and do His work in others, we use our finite words to invite an infinite God to do what we could never do. In His perfect sovereignty, God uses our prayers to move His mission forward. May we never neglect to pray for God to move in a person or situation, for He hears and responds to our prayers!

Finally, we know that we cannot overstate the importance of prayer in our lives because Jesus still prays for us continuously. Yes, Jesus has ascended to heaven and is sitting at the right hand of His Father. Yet the Bible tells us that He is still praying without ceasing (Romans 8:34, Hebrews 7:25). How precious and important must prayer be if it is the primary thing Jesus does even now!

When we look at the life of Jesus, we see a perfect picture of both passionate dedication to and the everyday practice of prayer. If we want to have a powerful prayer life, we must start by following in the intentional, prayerful footsteps of Jesus. We can do this by pushing aside the excuses and distractions and making time every day to speak with God through prayer. We should pray for God to unfold His perfect will in us and in the world around us. And we should never think that prayer is inconsequential because when we pray, we join Jesus in what He is doing at this very moment.

"

> God moves in response to prayer to do meaningful work in us and missional work in the world.

daily QUESTIONS

How would you describe your prayer life right now?
In what ways would you like to see your prayer life grow through this study?

How does examining Jesus's intentionality, missionality, and continuous practice of prayer impact you?

Which one of the above characteristics of Jesus's prayer life is the area you would like to grow in most? Why?

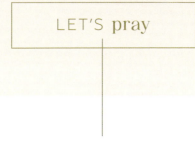

Write a prayer expressing your desire for
God to teach you to pray like Jesus.

Write a prayer asking God to show you places and times you can step away
from the busyness of life and be with Him.

Write a prayer that appeals for God to work in and through you to accomplish His will in the world.

_____
_____
_____
_____
_____
_____
_____
_____

"

If we want to have a powerful prayer life, we must start by following in the intentional, prayerful footsteps of Jesus.

Prayer is "an offering up of our desires unto God, for things agreeable to his will, in the name of Christ, with confession of our sins, and thankful acknowledgment of his mercies."

—THE WESTMINSTER CATECHISM

WEEK ONE
day 2

What is Prayer?

READ PSALM 62:8, 1 JOHN 5:14, JOHN 16:23-24, 1 JOHN 1:9, PSALM 103:1-5

You may have heard it said that prayer is merely talking to God. That is true, and there is no simpler definition of prayer than that. However, prayer is deeper and more dynamic than that short definition. If our understanding of prayer stops there, then we are missing out on the marvelous miracle and mystery that is communing with God Almighty.

The Westminster Catechism, a widely respected document that explains the theological foundation of the Christian faith, offers us a more robust explanation of what prayer is. It defines prayer as "an offering up of our desires unto God, for things agreeable to his will, in the name of Christ, with confession of our sins, and thankful acknowledgment of his mercies." This definition highlights five different aspects of prayer, and we will examine each one in today's study.

The first aspect of prayer is that it is *an offering up of our desires unto God*. We see this described beautifully in Psalm 62:8, where David depicts prayer as pouring out his heart before Him.

Our desires include our wants, needs, aches, pains, and deepest longings. Our hearts are full to the brim with desires. Prayer is a place to tip our full hearts over and let them spill out to God's listening ear. All desires are welcome in God's presence. But not all desires are granted. This brings us to the second aspect of prayer, *for things that are agreeable to his will*.

Can you imagine what the world would be like if God answered every single prayer with a "yes"? The momentary wishes of people would rule the world. Chaos would ensue. That is why God does not answer our prayers based on our desires but based on His will. God has a perfectly ordered and sovereignly executed will for every person in every millisecond.

When our prayers do not align with God's will, we can always expect Him to say no. But no one likes to receive "no" as an answer to their prayers. Many times, we do not understand why His will does not align with our desires. Yet, even in those moments, we can trust that His will is ultimately best for us. When God's "no's" are hard to comprehend, we can be comforted by two things. First, God's "yes" and His "no" are given because He is who He says He is, and He does what He says He will do. And second, when we delight in the Lord and His ways, He aligns our desires with His (Psalm 37:3). God does give us the desires of our hearts when our hearts are tuned to the frequency of His will—for it is then that our desires mirror His own for us (1 John 5:14).

The third aspect of prayer is *in the name of Christ*. To pray in the name of Christ not only means to add "in Jesus's name" to your prayers. It is much more about the motive behind the words than the words themselves.

It is helpful to understand the cultural context behind Jesus's instruction to His disciples to pray in His name in John 16:23-24. In biblical times, a person's name represented the whole of who they were and what they were like. So, to pray in the name of Christ means to pray in harmony with who Jesus is. "In Jesus's name" is not a magical phrase that unlocks God's willful grant of our request. It is more like a mold that shapes our prayers to be consistent with the character of Jesus.

Next is maybe the most beautiful of all the aspects of prayer—*with confession of sins*. The beauty in the confession part of prayer is that it is God's response to our initial confession of sin that leads to our salvation and, subsequently, unlimited access to God in prayer. But confession and asking forgiveness of sins is not a one-time thing. It is something we should practice continually.

As believers, we do not confess our sins because we have lost our salvation and need to earn it again. We confess our sins because God asks us to increasingly submit ourselves to Him so that He reigns over us and our sin does not (Romans 6:12-13). Therefore, we should daily confess our sins, ask for forgiveness, and plead with God to strengthen us so we can resist the temptation to sin in the future. When we confess, God forgives, and all is right between Him and us (1 John 1:9).

Because of His long-suffering forgiveness, we end with our last aspect of prayer—*thankful acknowledgment of his mercies*. We cannot help but be moved to tell the Lord how thankful we are for all of the loving-kindness He has lavished on us. After all, who is like the Lord? He forgives, heals, redeems, crowns us with His love, satisfies our souls, and renews us when we are weak. When we consider these things, how can we not say, "Bless the Lord, oh my soul, bless the Lord!" (Psalm 103:1-5).

Prayer is a beautiful, intricate exchange between us and God. Only through belief in Jesus and God's forgiveness of our sins can we enter into this type of communion. And once we enter into it, we have a lifetime of learning to pray ahead of us. As we deepen our understanding of prayer through this study, may it provoke in us a more emboldened and passionate prayer life than we have ever experienced!

daily QUESTIONS

How does today's study deepen your understanding of prayer?

Think about a time when God answered a prayer differently than you hoped or expected. What would it look like for you to trust that His will is better than your desires?

How does today's study change your view of what it means to pray "in Jesus's name?"

Write a prayer that pours out your heart's desires to the Lord.

Where are some areas you see sin in your own life and heart?
Write a prayer confessing these to the Lord and asking for His forgiveness.

How have you seen God working in your life this week?
Write a prayer thanking Him for the mercies He has granted you.

_____
_____
_____
_____
_____
_____
_____
_____
_____

"

Prayer is a beautiful, intricate exchange between us and God.

Remembering to whom we are praying is the first step of praying.

WEEK ONE

day 3

How Should I Pray?

READ MATTHEW 6:9-13, LUKE 11:1-4

Have you ever seen a couple on an awkward first date? They tend to stammer and stutter, accidentally talking over one another as they nervously try to keep the conversation going. Things only get worse when they run out of words, and a deafening silence sets in. It is at that moment they will find out if their relationship has a future or not. Will they push through, find common ground, and begin to build a friendship? Or will it fizzle to nothing?

We cannot compare God to the person sitting across from us on a first date; after all, He is our Maker, Creator, and Sustainer. He knows us better than we know ourselves. But sometimes, our prayer life can feel like those clumsy first-date conversations. What should we say? What if we run out of words? Why does it sometimes feel awkward to pray?

Thankfully, Jesus teaches us how to pray in Matthew 6:9-13, and when we practice following the guidelines He gives us, we can grow to have a rich and vibrant prayer life! This passage is frequently called The Lord's Prayer, and its words may be familiar to you. It is important to note that Jesus did not say that this prayer should be recited word for word. He starts by saying, "you should pray like this." He is giving us an example and a pattern to follow. You certainly can recite this prayer, but Jesus gave it to us as a guideline that we can each use to pray with our own words.

The Lord's prayer contains four phrases that we will study to learn how Jesus wants us to pray. The first two phrases in this prayer focus on the worthiness and holiness of God. The second two phrases focus on the personal needs of believers.

Our Father in heaven, your name be honored as holy.

The beauty of this short sentence is hard to convey. It was not normal to refer to God as Father in Jesus's time. He was breaking protocol and suggesting a warm and intimate relationship by addressing God as Father. Yet, at the same time, He reminds us that God resides in heaven. He is set apart, holy, and ruling sovereignly over the world. We have a wonderfully personal relationship with an infinitely awesome God.

Remembering to whom we are praying is the first step of praying. Otherwise, prayer can become just listing your grievances aloud, or even worse, having a conversation with yourself. When you begin to pray, choose to address the Lord in a way that honors who He is and reminds you of who He is in your life.

Your kingdom come, your will be done, on earth as it is in heaven.

These phrases focus on the central mission given to all Christians—to expand the kingdom of God on the earth. God's kingdom on this earth is not a physical place, but rather it is being built in the hearts of people who love and serve Him. We should ask God to continue to build His kingdom in and through us.

And then we pray for God's will to be done. When we do this, we are not praying for a secret, mysterious will that has not been shown to us but for God's revealed will in Scripture to come to pass. God's revealed will is found on every page and in every verse in all of the Bible. It is full of wisdom, counsel, revelation, and truth that guide us to walk in the will of God. And we should pray that God's will—as according to Scripture—be done in the world.

Give us this day our daily bread, and forgive us our debts, as we also have forgiven our debtors.

Now Jesus's guide to prayer shifts from being God-focused to being focused on the personal needs of the one praying. The phrase "daily bread" does not just refer to bread, it is a reference to all of the physical needs one has in a day. How reassuring to know Jesus wants us to bring our daily needs to the Father! He also adds a prayer of restoration and forgiveness for the sins we commit that hold back our relationship with God. And finally, He reminds us that because we have been forgiven, we also must forgive others.

And do not bring us into temptation, but deliver us from the evil one.

The final phrase of Jesus's prayer is for our spiritual well-being. Jesus concludes His prayer by asking God for closeness to Him. We should pray that God prevents us from being in situations where we might sin and pray that He protects us from the plans of Satan. By closing His prayer in this way, Jesus reminds us that what we need is to be near to God and far from sin.

The Lord's prayer shows us the chief aim of prayer—to glorify God, commune with God, partner with God, and ask for the providence and help of God. Jesus taught the Lord's Prayer as a guide for us. And, when filled with our individual words, this prayer will lead us into a dynamic and enjoyable prayer life. More than that, Jesus gave His life as a sacrifice for our sins so we could come into a relationship with God and enter into a meaningful prayer life! Jesus taught us to pray and made a way for us to pray. He is the means by which we pray!

daily QUESTIONS

God is a loving Father with whom we can have a close and intimate relationship. Reflect on your relationship with God, and write out what kind of a Father He is.

Read Exodus 16. What correlations do you see between manna and Jesus's prayer for the provision of daily bread? How does this inform the way you ask God for your daily bread?

Which of the four sections of the Lord's prayer above is most neglected in your prayer life? How might your prayer life change if you focused on developing that area of prayer?

LET'S pray

For the remainder of the study, we will use the Lord's Prayer as a guide for our daily times of prayer. You can always expand upon this guide, and we will often tailor it to the daily study topics. As we pray in this pattern daily for the next several weeks, the hope is that this helps you establish a biblical framework for a practical and passionate prayer life.

Our Father: Choose two or three of your favorite attributes of God (refer to the Attributes of God on Pages 6-7 if needed), and write a prayer praising God for how He embodies each of these attributes.

_____
_____
_____
_____
_____

Your Kingdom Come: Write a prayer expressing your desire for God to build His kingdom and accomplish His will in your life and the world.

_____
_____
_____
_____
_____

Daily Bread: What are your physical needs today? Write a prayer asking God to meet them.

_____
_____
_____
_____
_____

Forgive Our Sins: *Take a moment to confess, and ask forgiveness for sins you have committed. As you receive God's forgiveness, remember that He has called you to forgive others.*

_____
_____
_____
_____

Deliver Us: *Write a prayer asking God to help you avoid sin and stay close to Him.*

_____
_____
_____
_____
_____

"

Jesus gave His life as a sacrifice for our sins so we could come into a relationship with God and enter into a meaningful prayer life!

Even when prayer does not seem to change the world around us, God uses it to change us.

WEEK ONE

day 4

Do My Prayers Matter?

READ 1 THESSALONIANS 5:16-18, PSALM 16:11, JOHN 16:24, MATTHEW 26:41, JAMES 4:2

Have you ever asked yourself...

What is the point in praying for what I want if God knows best?
If God already knows the future, why do my prayers matter today?
Is it pointless for me to pray if God is going to do what He wants no matter what?

If so, you are not alone! It can feel pointless to pray when we compare our seemingly small prayers to an infinitely large God who acts according to His sovereign will. But prayer is not pointless! We pray out of obedience and for the joy it brings. We pray so that God can transform us through the process. And we pray to fill our role in the God-designed partnership of prayer. Let us further examine each of these reasons our prayers matter.

We pray out of obedience.

According to the Bible, prayer is not optional, and therefore, we should pray even when we do not want to and even when we question whether it will have an effect. Verses like 1 Thessalonians 5:16-18 tell us that to pray constantly is God's will for our lives! And Deuteronomy 10:13 tells us that it is for our good to keep God's commands.

We pray for the joy of it.

The first reason our prayer matters is because we do it out of obedience. And that is reason enough, but thankfully, the reasons to pray do not end there. We also pray for the joy of it! In Psalm 16:11, the psalmist tells us in God's presence, there is "fullness of joy," and at His right hand are "eternal pleasures."

When we enter into prayer, center our thoughts on the Lord, and submit our requests to Him, we are living in His presence. And joy is one of the results. We also learn in John 16:24 that we should pray because we receive joy from answered prayers. Jesus says, "Ask and you will receive, so that your joy may be complete."

We pray so God can transform us through it.

Sometimes prayers seem to go unanswered, and rather than feeling joy, we feel frustration or confusion. We should pray in these times because it transforms us to become more like Christ and aligns our desires with God's desires. Even when prayer does not seem to change the world around us, God uses it to change us. When Jesus was praying in the garden of Gethsemane just before His crucifixion, He asked His disciples to stay awake and pray with Him because He was in great agony. However, the disciples repeatedly fell asleep.

Jesus's response was, "Stay awake and pray, so that you won't enter into temptation. The spirit is willing, but the flesh is weak" (Matthew 26:41). The disciples were neglecting to pray because of the weakness of their flesh and their proneness to sin. Jesus said that the answer to overcoming this weakness was to pray. Just like the disciples in this example, God uses prayer to help us become more like Christ.

We pray to fill our role in the God-designed partnership of prayer.

The last reason we should pray is shrouded in mystery. God, who is sovereign, listens to and responds to our prayers. He listens! How incredible! God is ultimately sovereign, but He has chosen to let us enter into a God-designed yet mysterious partnership with Him in which our prayers have a place in how He works in the world. This does not mean that our prayers change His mind or His plans. It simply means that He is powerful enough to know His plans and the prayers we will pray. And He works it all together in a way that only He can.

James 4:2 says, "You do not have because you do not ask." Our prayers have a place in the partnership of prayer. To neglect prayer is to neglect taking part in the most astonishing relationship available to us. Prayer is a gift—a marvelous mystery. The Bible gives us no reason to believe that our prayers are meaningless. It matters when you pray in obedience. It matters when you pray for the joy of it. It matters that you are inwardly transformed into the likeness of Christ through prayer. And it matters that God allows your prayers to partner with Him to accomplish His good and perfect will in the world. Your prayers matter.

Prayer is a gift—a marvelous mystery.

Which of the reasons prayer matters stuck out to you most?
How does it change your approach to prayer?

When prayer does not change the world around us, God is likely using it to change us. How does this encourage you in your own prayer life?

What would it look like for you to take your role in the partnership of prayer seriously?

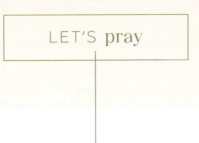

LET'S pray

Let's pray using the format we learned yesterday from The Lord's Prayer. As you are writing your prayers, keep in mind that the words you pray matter. Pray passionately, with thanksgiving and joy, and believe that the words you pray will cause a change in you or in the world around you.

Our Father: Write a prayer praising God for how the gift of prayer displays His goodness toward us. Praise God for any other attributes (on pages 6-7) He possesses that came to mind as you read today's study.

_____
_____
_____
_____
_____

Your Kingdom Come: Write a prayer expressing your desire for God to build His kingdom and accomplish His will in your life and the world through the prayers you pray.

_____
_____
_____
_____
_____

Daily Bread: What are your physical needs today? Write a prayer asking God to meet them.

_____
_____
_____
_____
_____

Forgive Our Sins: *Take a moment to confess, and ask forgiveness for sins you have committed. Today, this may include not obeying God's command to pray. As you receive God's forgiveness, remember that He has called you to forgive others.*

_____
_____
_____
_____

Deliver Us: *Write a prayer asking God to help you avoid sin and stay close to Him.*

_____
_____
_____
_____

"

When we enter into prayer, center our thoughts on the Lord, and submit our requests to Him, we are living in His presence.

Jesus is the "yes" we all need most, and God has provided Him for us according to His perfect will.

WEEK ONE

day 5

The Ways God Answers Prayer

READ ACTS 28:7-10, 1 SAMUEL 1, 2 CORINTHIANS 12:7-10

If you have ever sat in stunned silence after God answered your prayer with a "no" or "not yet," then you are in good company. Or maybe your response was not silence but rather groaning in sorrow or loud outbursts of frustration. There is a chorus of others who have joined you in that place as well.

You may have also experienced the joy and exuberance that overtakes you when God answers a precious prayer with a "yes!" God's answers to prayer tend to invoke deep emotions from us because our prayers are often so important to us. We can be assured that God always answers our prayers, but He does not always answer them the way we want.

In Scripture, we see that God answers prayers in three main ways: "yes," "not yet," and "no." Let us examine more closely each of these answers to prayer to understand how God uses them for His glory and our good.

— *Yes* —

In Acts 28:1-10, Paul lands ashore of Malta after being shipwrecked. He is immediately bitten by a poisonous snake, which he survives by a miracle of God. Then he comes to the home of Publius, the chief officer of the island, and realizes that Publius's father is ill and bedridden. Paul prays, and immediately the man is healed and made well!

God's answer was an immediate yes to Paul's prayer for healing. While it is not detailed what happened in the hearts of the people of Malta as a response to this healing, we know that many came to Paul and were also healed, which leads us to believe they had faith in God. And we know that Paul was dedicated to spreading the gospel and likely shared the good news of Jesus with the people as well.

The Maltese honored Paul and blessed him with as many provisions as he needed when he left the island. The healing of Publius's father glorified God and brought good to Paul. A "yes" answer is always the easiest in which to see our good and the glory of God. But what about a "not yet"? Can we see good and glory there?

— *Not Yet* —

Hannah's story of longing for a child in 1 Samuel 1 shows us how God works in long periods of waiting for a yes. Hannah was barren, bullied by her husband's other (and more fruitful) wife, and begged God year after year for a child. Her grief over her barrenness was so great that Hannah "would weep and would not eat" (1 Samuel 1:7). But Hannah never stops praying. And her persistent prayers end with a son in her arms. Before her son Samuel was conceived, Hannah vowed if the Lord gave her a son, she would give him to the Lord all the days of his life.

Hannah kept her vow, and after he was weaned, Samuel was raised in the temple and trained to be a priest in the service of the Lord. Samuel had an impressive impact on Israel and served as a priest, prophet, and judge until his death. He was an instrumental leader of the nation, both spiritually and politically. He anointed Saul as the first king of Israel as the Lord commanded and then anointed David as the king who would replace Saul.

Samuel's life was perfectly placed in a tumultuous time. Hannah's prayers seemed unanswered for years on end, but God planned the exact time and place that her son would be born all along. God's "not yet" was for the good of all Israel and His glory that would be made known through the life of Samuel.

— *No* —

Finally, we come to the most difficult answer God can give us—no. You may have experienced being told "no" by God. Even the heroes of the Christian faith experienced this. In 2 Corinthians 12:7-10, Paul prays for God to remove a "thorn in the flesh."

Whatever the thorn was, it obviously hindered Paul's ability to travel and preach the gospel. It seems logical that God would remove it so that Paul could spread the message farther and wider. But Paul pleads with the Lord three times, and three times the Lord says "no." Paul never received earthly relief from his thorn in the flesh. He did, however, receive power from Christ to overcome his weaknesses.

God answered "no" because it glorified Him for Paul to be weak. In his weakness, Christ's power shined all the more brilliantly through him. While it certainly was not comfortable for Paul to have a persistent thorn in the flesh, he does let us know that this thorn kept him humble. 2 Corinthians 12:7 says, "so that I would not exalt myself, a thorn in the flesh was given to me." And James 4:6 says, "God resists the proud, but gives grace to the humble." Paul's thorn kept him humble, which allowed God to give him further grace. Although it may not have been the answer Paul chose, he was blessed through it.

When God answers our prayers, we often compare His given answer to our desired answer. God is big enough to handle our questions and frustrations about His answers. But rather than letting us sit and stew on what we perceive He should have done, He will usually answer those questions by reminding us to trust His character and the fact that He works all things for good. Whether it is a "yes," "not yet," or a "no," a better approach to understanding why God answers our prayers the way He does is to search for God's glory and our good in the answer we have been given.

No matter how often He answers "no," we have the assurance that He has answered "yes" to our greatest need–the need for a Savior to rescue us from our sin and bring us into a relationship with Him. Jesus is the "yes" we all need most, and God has provided Him for us according to His perfect will.

daily QUESTIONS

Think of a recent prayer you prayed that God seemingly answered with a "no" or "not yet." How can you see the glory of God and your good through this answer? Be honest. It is okay if you cannot yet see these things.

How does Hannah's story of the birth of Samuel encourage you to keep praying for prayers that seem to be going unanswered?

Are you sitting and stewing on an answer God has given you? How can you begin to trust the Lord with that answer?

LET'S pray

Let today's Bible reading and study specifically influence your prayers. Avoid reciting the same prayer every day, but bring today's praises and problems to God through this guide.

Our Father: *Write a prayer praising God for being just and righteous. Refer to the descriptions of these attributes on pages 6-7.*

_____
_____
_____
_____
_____

Your Kingdom Come: *Write a prayer expressing your desire for God to build His kingdom and accomplish His will in your life and the world, even if that means God does not answer your prayers in the way you desire.*

_____
_____
_____
_____
_____

Daily Bread: *What are your physical needs today? Write a prayer asking God to meet them.*

_____
_____
_____
_____
_____

Forgive Our Sins: *Take a moment to confess, and ask forgiveness for sins you have committed. As you receive God's forgiveness, remember that He has called you to forgive others.*

_____
_____
_____
_____
_____

Deliver Us: *Write a prayer asking God to help you avoid sin and stay close to Him.*

_____
_____
_____
_____
_____

God is big enough to handle our questions and frustrations about His answers.

Therefore, you should pray like this: Our Father in heaven, your name be honored as holy. Your kingdom come. Your will be done on earth as it is in heaven. Give us today our daily bread. And forgive us our debts, as we also have forgiven our debtors. And do not bring us into temptation, but deliver us from the evil one.

MATTHEW 6:9-13

weekly REFLECTION

Review all Scripture passages from the week.

Summarize the main points from this week's Scripture readings.

What did you observe from this week's passages about God and His character?

What do this week's passages reveal about the condition of mankind and yourself?

WEEK ONE

How do these passages point to the gospel?

How should you respond to these Scriptures? What specific action steps can you take this week to apply them in your life?

Write a prayer in response to your study of God's Word. Adore God for who He is, confess sins He revealed in your own life, ask Him to empower you to walk in obedience, and pray for anyone who comes to mind as you study.

Aggie Hurst's Story

David and Svea Flood felt God's call to move from Sweden to N'dolera, a remote part of the Belgian Congo (now the Democratic Republic of Congo) as missionaries in 1912. They arrived with their two-year-old son, eager to build relationships and share the gospel with the Congolese in a village called N'dolera. But the village chief refused them entry to the village and forbade anyone from speaking to them except a young boy who was allowed to sell them eggs and chickens once a week. They were greatly discouraged by this, but Svea decided that if the only person she could talk to was this little boy, she would win him to Christ. And she did!

Svea then became pregnant, and when it was time to give birth, she struggled greatly because her body was already weak from continuous battles with malaria. She gave birth to a little girl named Aina, and then Svea died seventeen days later. David was devastated and could no longer cope. He buried his 27-year-old wife then took his children back to their missionary base at the bottom of the rural mountain on which they had been living. He gave the baby girl to another missionary couple and said, "I'm going back to Sweden. God has ruined my life."

Tragically, Aina's new caretakers also became ill and died only months later. She was then given to yet another missionary couple who nicknamed her "Aggie" and took her home to the United States. Aggie grew up and married a Christian man who became the president of a Christian college.

One day a Swedish magazine appeared in her mailbox, and in it was a picture of a grave with a white cross with Svea Flood written on it. Stunned, she took the magazine to a college professor who spoke Swedish and asked him to translate it for her.

The article detailed the story of a missionary woman who had led a boy to Christ before her tragic death. The boy had grown and started a school in the village where he led all of his students to Christ. They led their parents to Christ, and eventually, even the chief believed. There were now 600 Christians in that tiny, remote village thanks to the prayers and efforts of Svea Flood.

After this incredible realization, Aggie sought out her birth father in Sweden, who was ill, an alcoholic, and still bitterly angry with God. She arranged a meeting with him and told him the story of the impact of their time spent praying and interacting with the people of N'dolera. He wept. And after decades of anger toward God, his heart softened, and his faith was restored. He died a short time later.

A few years later, Aggie and her husband attended a worldwide evangelism conference in London. A man shared about the spread of Christianity in Zaire, formerly the Belgian Congo and currently the Democratic Republic of Congo. The man said there were 110,000 baptized believers in the country. Aggie wanted to meet this man and see if, by chance, he knew of her parents. When she met with him, she asked him this question, and he replied, "Yes, madam. It was Svea Flood who led me to Christ. I was the little boy who brought food to your parents before you were born." Aggie hugged the man tightly and sobbed. Eventually, she was able to visit Zaire and see her mother's grave. Although her mother had died and all hope seemed lost at the time, her parents' prayers for the Congolese people were abundantly answered.

"There were now 600 Christians in that tiny, remote village thanks to the prayers and efforts of Svea Flood."

WEEK TWO

going deeper

BUILDING ON PRAYER FOUNDATIONS

Now that we have a better understanding of the basics of prayer, it is time to answer some deeper questions about prayer and how it works.

Will God give me the things I ask for in prayer?
What is the Holy Spirit's role in prayer?
How can I best pray for the people I love?
Can I pray for anything I want?
How important is it to praise God in times of prayer?

This week, we will search Scripture to find solid, biblical answers to these questions. We may need to unlearn things we believed as a child. Or we may be surprised to learn something new we have never seen before in Scripture. As a result, we will understand more deeply God's very good design for prayer.

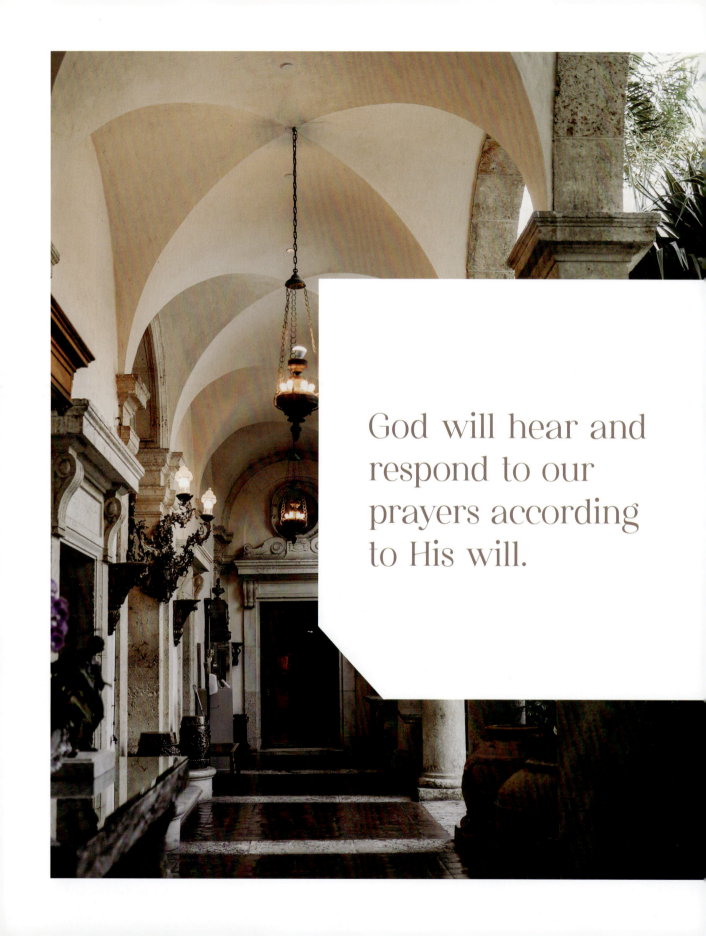

God will hear and respond to our prayers according to His will.

WEEK TWO

day 1

Have Faith and Don't Doubt

READ JAMES 1:5-8, PSALM 103:12-14, MARK 9:17-29, MATTHEW 21:18-22

Can you imagine getting on a plane if you believed it was not possible for such a large aircraft to fly? Or getting on a boat if you did not believe the boat could float on water? If you genuinely believed that planes could not fly and boats could not float, you would never step aboard either of them. There would be too much risk and no reward. In much the same way, the Bible instructs us to enter into prayer with the belief that God is real, good, and active on our behalf. We must pray with faith.

One of the most compelling passages on praying with faith is James 1:6-8, which reads, "But let him ask in faith without doubting. For the doubter is like the surging sea, driven and tossed by the wind. That person should not expect to receive anything from the Lord, being double-minded and unstable in all his ways." What strong words we find here for those who pray in doubt and not in faith—*that person should not expect to receive anything from the Lord.*

What if we want to have faith, but it feels impossible? What if a doubtful thought enters our mind as we are praying? Does that nullify the prayer? These are all important questions to answer if we want to pray prayers to which God responds.

First, be assured that God's character is unchanging toward those who love and serve Him. We see God's heart described beautifully in Psalm 103:13-14, "As a father has compassion on his children, so the Lord has compassion on those who fear him. For he knows what we are made of, remembering that we are dust."

God does not require a perfect faith that never has fleeting moments of doubt. No, the doubter referenced in James 1:6 is someone who makes the willful decision to place their trust in both the Lord and themselves. This person is described as double-minded or maybe more accurately double-souled. They want God in small doses. They may sparingly sprinkle Him on the places in their life that feel incomplete or above their paygrade, but they are not interested in wholeheartedly and single-mindedly serving Him. Ultimately, the root of this kind of relationship with God is an absence of faith in God.

Second, we need to know what this passage does not mean. It does not mean we should suppress or sweep under the rug feelings of doubt that enter our mind as we are praying or any other time. God is not angry with us when we have momentary distrust. When we begin to nurture thoughts of distrust and allow them to draw us from dependence on God to dependence on self, we become double-minded and faithless. To avoid this, we should bring these thoughts out into the light of God's presence and cry, "I do believe; help my unbelief!" (Mark 9:24).

This portion of Scripture also does not mean we should pray expecting to receive exactly that for which we have been praying. This passage has commonly been taken out of context to teach this. Faith's object of trust can never be an outcome or a thing. It can only be God.

And finally, here is what this passage does mean: It means that faith in God, not in an outcome, is a firm foundation on which we can stand as we pray. When we doubt, we and our prayers are unstable. If we do not believe that God is good, listening, and active in response to our prayers then why pray? Those faithless prayers leave us tossed by the billows and gasping for breath as we send our prayer into the abyss. But if we commit ourselves wholeheartedly to the Lord, confess unbelief when it arises, and cling to the truths of God we find in His Word, then God will hear and respond to our prayers according to His will.

Faith is an essential component of prayer. Jesus Himself addresses this in Matthew 21:22 when he says, "And if you believe, you will receive whatever you ask for in prayer." Faith in Jesus is necessary for our salvation, and faith in God is necessary in our prayers. If we do not truly believe, then we are praying to nothing and no one. But if we believe in Jesus, receive God's forgiveness, and pray with faith, then we are praying to our Lord and Savior! Let us believe in God, pray earnestly to Him, and await our receiving of His perfect answer to our prayers.

Faith is an essential component of prayer.

daily QUESTIONS

Take a moment to examine your own heart. When you pray, do you pray in faith?

What can you do when you experience doubt in God to remain single-mindedly devoted to the Lord?

Faith's object of trust can never be an outcome or a thing. It can only be God. How can you be sure you are placing your faith in the Lord and not in the outcome you want from your prayers?

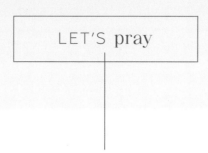

Let today's Bible reading and study specifically influence your prayers. Avoid reciting the same prayer every day, but bring today's praises and problems to God through this guide.

Our Father: *What attributes remind you that God is worthy of your faith in Him? Write a prayer praising God for embodying these attributes. Refer to the list of attributes on page 6-7 if needed.*

_____
_____
_____
_____
_____

Your Kingdom Come: *Write a prayer expressing your desire for God to build His kingdom and accomplish His will in your life and the world. Express your faith in His ability to accomplish these things.*

_____
_____
_____
_____
_____

Daily Bread: *What are your physical needs today? Write a prayer asking God to meet them and let Him know you trust Him to meet them.*

_____
_____
_____
_____
_____

Forgive Our Sins: *Take a moment to confess, and ask forgiveness for sins you have committed. As you receive God's forgiveness, remember that He has called you to forgive others.*

Deliver Us: *Write a prayer asking God to help you avoid sin and stay close to Him.*

"

God does not require a perfect faith that never has fleeting moments of doubt.

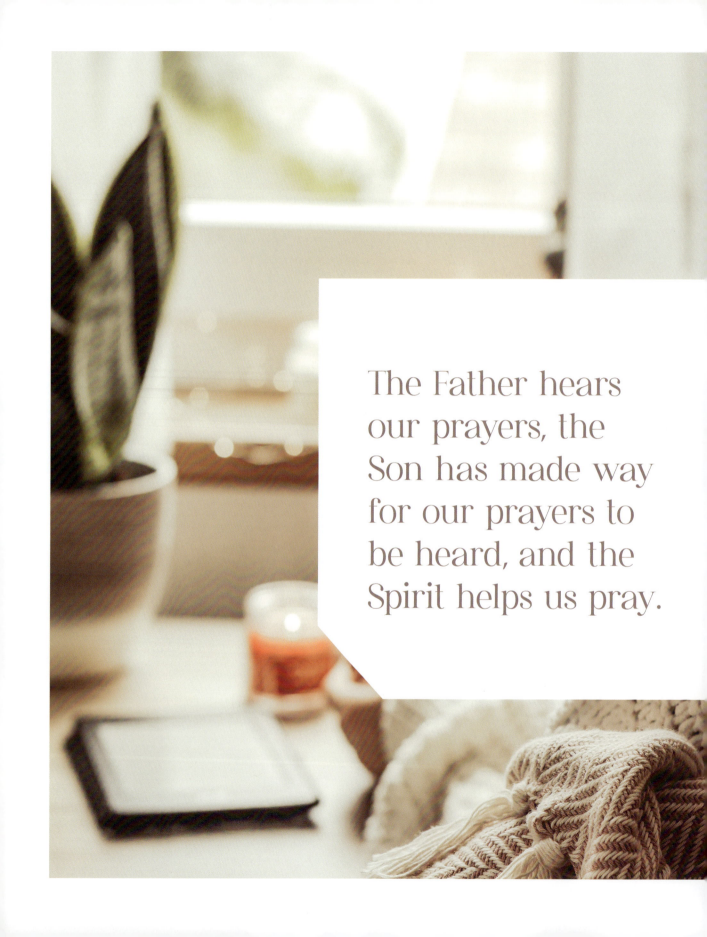

The Father hears our prayers, the Son has made way for our prayers to be heard, and the Spirit helps us pray.

WEEK TWO

day 2

Prayer and the Holy Spirit

READ ROMANS 8:26-27, EPHESIANS 6:17-19, JOHN 4:23-24, JUDE 1:20

The Holy Spirit. He is likely the most misunderstood member of the Trinity. He is as much God as God the Father and Jesus the Son, yet His role is different from theirs. His role in prayer is unique, and we cannot have a full understanding of prayer without knowing what His role is in it. The Holy Spirit's role in prayer can be seen as mystical and mysterious, but Scripture clarifies His role telling us that He is our help in prayer.

Simply put, the Father hears our prayers, the Son has made way for our prayers to be heard, and the Spirit helps us pray. This is illustrated by a few key passages; one is Romans 8:26-27.

> In the same way the Spirit also helps us in our weakness, because we do not know what to pray for as we should, but the Spirit himself intercedes for us with inexpressible groanings. And he who searches our hearts knows the mind of the Spirit, because he intercedes for the saints according to the will of God.

Similar to the way Jesus sits at the right hand of God in heaven and intercedes for all believers, the Holy Spirit also intercedes for us. But He intercedes on our behalf from His place of residence—in our hearts. He does not do this audibly but with inexpressible groanings. This does not mean unintelligible talk, such as the gift of tongues, but rather that the Spirit who has no physical being and is omnipresent, omnipotent, and omniscient communicates without words in the way only the Spirit can. These profoundly personal prayers the Spirit lifts to the Father on our behalf are such a great help to us because they always fully and completely align with the perfect will of God.

Let us make this more practical. When you are faced with a deeply distressing situation, and you find that the only prayer you can utter is, "God, help!" the Holy Spirit, who is God residing in you, boldly lifts prayers perfectly in line with God's will for you. He helps you pray when you are weak. The Holy Spirit prays for you to the God (Father) who hears you through the God (Jesus) who has brought you into this perfect triune God union. Jesus also intercedes for all believers to the Father. The Trinity (God, Jesus, and the Holy Spirit) is a constant triune prayer meeting!

We also see in Scripture that we are commanded to "pray in the Spirit" (Ephesians 6:18, Jude 1:20). This, again, does not refer to the spiritual gift of speaking in tongues. Rather, it is a reference to praying, aware of and tuned to the leading of the Holy Spirit. And how does the Holy Spirit lead us? He leads us according to what Jesus has spoken and what is written in God's Word. John 14:26 tells us, "But the Counselor, the Holy Spirit, whom the Father will send in my name, will teach you all things and remind you of everything I have told you." And He leads the depths of us, even parts that are hidden from our own view, to come into alignment with the depths of God: "Now God has revealed these things to us by the Spirit, since the Spirit searches everything, even the depths of God. For who knows a person's thoughts except his spirit within him? In the same way, no one knows the thoughts of God except the Spirit of God" (1 Corinthians 2:10-11).

The Holy Spirit's role in prayer is not strange or scary. It is profound and personal. He leads us to God, He knows God's will and prays it for us, and He helps us pray when we are weak. The Holy Spirit is a divine intercessor that lives and moves in us. His role in prayer is vital! But the Holy Spirit only works in our prayer life if we have been brought into a relationship with God through faith in Jesus. Then, through Jesus's payment for our sins, we will be brought into a relationship with God, filled with the Holy Spirit, and given the ability to pray!

> The Holy Spirit is a divine intercessor that lives and moves in us.

daily QUESTIONS

How does today's study inform who the Holy Spirit is and what His role is in your prayer life?

How do you feel knowing the Holy Spirit personally and perfectly intercedes for you even when you do not know what to pray for yourself?

How have you experienced the Holy Spirit leading you to align your thoughts, actions, and prayers with God's will?

LET'S pray

Let today's Bible reading and study specifically influence your prayers. Avoid reciting the same prayer every day, but bring today's praises and problems to God through this guide.

Our Father: *Refer to the list of attributes on pages 6-7. Write a prayer praising God (Father, Son, and Holy Spirit) for embodying one or more of these attributes.*

_____
_____
_____
_____

Your Kingdom Come: *Write a prayer expressing your desire for God to build His kingdom and accomplish His will in your life and the world. Ask the Holy Spirit to help you partner with God in the accomplishing of His will.*

_____
_____
_____
_____

Daily Bread: *What are your physical needs today? Write a prayer asking God to meet them and let Him know you trust Him to meet them.*

_____
_____
_____
_____

Forgive Our Sins: *Take a moment to confess, and ask forgiveness for sins you have committed. As you receive God's forgiveness, remember that He has called you to forgive others.*

_____
_____
_____
_____
_____

Deliver Us: *Write a prayer asking God to help you avoid sin and stay close to Him. Thank the Holy Spirit for being a help to you in this.*

_____
_____
_____
_____
_____

"

The Holy Spirit only works in our prayer life if we have been brought into a relationship with God through faith in Jesus.

The Trinity

The word "Trinity" means "three in one," and it describes the nature of God. This doctrine is a primary doctrine of the Christian faith. God is three persons, the Father, the Son, and the Holy Spirit, perfectly united in one essence. The three persons of the Trinity are fully God. They are distinct from one another, exist simultaneously, and are also perfectly united to one another. All three members of the Trinity have existed, in perfect love and communion with one another, for all of eternity.

Because the three members of the Trinity dwell within each other and are perfectly united, we can trust that they always act consistently with one another. The Father will never contradict the Son, who will never contradict the Spirit. For this reason, we can trust the work and revelation of the members of the Trinity in Scripture, and we can rest in confidence that God does not contradict Himself. He is fully trustworthy.

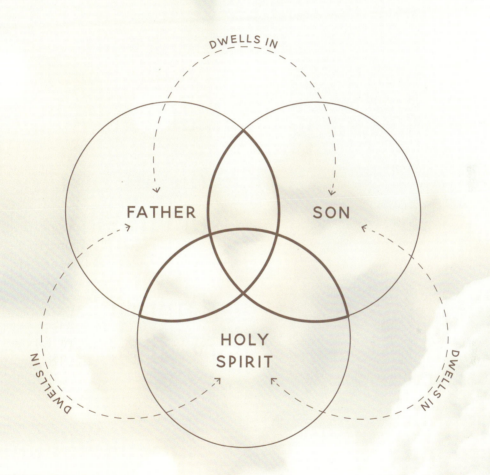

We can bring every desire, whether major or minor, to God in prayer.

WEEK TWO

day 3

Praying for Wants and Needs

READ PSALM 37:4, PSALM 84:11, MATTHEW 6:7-8, MATTHEW 7:9-11

The most pressing prayer requests in our hearts and minds change over our lifetime. Some days we beg on bent knees for divine healing, and other days, we just want to enjoy nice weather over the weekend. There are times when we simply want God to help us find our lost keys, and then there are times when we petition for our spiritually lost child to return to faith. Does God hear all of these requests? Should we pray for small or seemingly trivial things? Does God listen to both our needs and our wants?

The simple answer to all of these questions is "yes." God is big enough to handle every request we send His way. He is not so taxed by tending to those sick and destitute that He cannot help with more mundane petitions. God is without limit. We need only read Job 40-42 or Psalm 139 to remember that God is infinitely strong, and there is nothing too hard for Him. To limit our prayers because we think God may have better things to tend to is to believe that the limitless God has met His limit.

However, when we pray for our wants and needs, we are given guidelines on how we should and should not pray. In Matthew 6:7-8, we are told what not to do. We should not pray mindlessly or ritualistically. At the time Jesus spoke these words, it was a common pagan practice to repeat phrases over and over in an attempt to be noticed and elicit a response from pagan gods. Perhaps this became a practice because people realized their prayers to carved and cast idols were going unanswered, and so they began praying longer prayers more often.

We, however, are not praying to a worthless image but the one and only Creator. We do not need to attempt to earn His attention by talking in a certain way or for a certain amount of time. When we come to God with a need or a want, we are talking to someone who is already intimately aware of every detail, small and large, of our life. He is not unaware, but He is waiting for us to bring our needs to Him in prayer. We should ask, believing that God is accessible to us and invested in us—because He is.

A good earthly father loves to meet the needs of his child. Matthew 7:9-10 says that it is unnatural for a father to give a child a stone if he asks for bread or a serpent if he asks for fish. What mean and cruel tricks to play on a hungry child! And yet, God is so much more kind, wise, available, and loving than any earthly father. Verse 11 asks, "how much more will your Father in heaven give good things to those who ask Him?" Unbelievably more.

The only boundaries God has for giving good gifts to those who ask is His character and will. He will never give anything that is outside His will or against His character. We see this explained in Psalm 37:4, which says, "Take delight in the Lord, and he will give you your heart's desires." And we see it again in Psalm 84:11: "he does not withhold the good from those who live with integrity."

When we pray for the things God wills, we can be assured that the wants and needs we pray for will be given to us. And when we do not pray in accordance with His will and character, He will answer with a no, and that is for our good. We can never know His will perfectly before we pray, so we must trust that His answers align with His will, even when they do not align with ours.

The process of being brought into alignment with God's will begins when we believe Jesus Christ is Lord and ask for God to forgive our sins. God is faithful to forgive, we are saved from eternal death, and the process of growing in godliness begins in us. God initiates this process, Jesus makes it possible, and the Holy Spirit works continually in us each and every day.

We do not have to perfectly discern His will before we pray, but as we study Scripture and learn His revealed will, our prayers should reflect an ever-increasing arc of praying within His will. We can bring every desire, whether major or minor, to God in prayer. And we should! He will answer according to His will and ways. We need only ask our loving Father, who will lovingly respond, whether with a "yes" or a "no."

"

> When we come to God with a need or a want, we are talking to someone who is already intimately aware of every detail, small and large, of our life.

daily QUESTIONS

Do you ever hesitate to bring your wants or needs to God? Why or why not?

How can you be sure your prayers are genuine, not full of empty phrases?

How can you know and pray the revealed will of God?

LET'S pray

Let today's Bible reading and study specifically influence your prayers. Avoid reciting the same prayer every day, but bring today's praises and problems to God through this guide.

Our Father: Refer to the list of attributes on pages 6-7. Write a prayer praising God for answering our prayers with grace and love.

Your Kingdom Come: Write a prayer expressing your desire for God to build His kingdom and accomplish His will in your life and the world.

Daily Bread: What are your physical needs today? Write a prayer asking God to meet them. Include a prayer for your big and small wants as well.

Forgive Our Sins: *Take a moment to confess, and ask forgiveness for sins you have committed. As you receive God's forgiveness, remember that He has called you to forgive others.*

_____
_____
_____
_____

Deliver Us: *Write a prayer asking God to help you avoid sin and stay close to Him.*

_____
_____
_____
_____
_____

> "
>
> To limit our prayers because we think God may have better things to tend to is to believe that the limitless God has met His limit.

The most urgent thing we can pray for others is for their salvation.

WEEK TWO

day 4

Praying for People You Love

READ EPHESIANS 3:14-21, MATTHEW 6:9-14

Other than yourself, who do you pray for most? The answer is probably that you pray for those closest and dearest to you. It could be your child who is navigating a challenging time, a friend who recently experienced a loss, or a spouse who has wandered away from their faith in God. The lives of our friends and family are outside our control, and we often find ourselves bringing our requests for protection and peace before the Lord on their behalf. But, according to Scripture, there may be a better way to pray for the ones we love.

Let's consider the Lord's Prayer model we have used to pray throughout this study. We see that Jesus certainly includes physical needs when He teaches us to pray for our "daily bread," but the vast majority of the prayer is not about our circumstantial life but our spiritual life. In the same way, an emphasis on praying for others by focusing on spiritual matters more than physical needs is seen throughout the New Testament, especially in the prayers of Paul of which we have many recorded in the epistles.

When we examine the prayers Paul prayed for his beloved children of the faith, we find that he prayed prayers that are far beyond the surface level and circumstantial. This does not mean we should not pray for peace and prosperity for our loved ones, but it does mean we should take note of Paul's prayers and, as a result, deepen the scope of the prayers we pray.

In Ephesians 3:14-19, Paul prays for the believers at Ephesus. His prayer cuts straight to the heart of things. He makes no requests for any of their physical needs but instead points to this one aim—that the Ephesian believers would be filled with all the fullness of God. Is this not what we desire most for our loved ones? We want them to have joy, peace, contentment, and love. We may pray for earthly measures of these things, but would we be better off praying for divine doses instead?

Paul's prayer includes several specific things that together account for being filled with the fullness of God. He prays that Christ would dwell in their hearts or for their belief in Christ and subsequent salvation. He prays for inner strength according to the inexhaustible riches of God. He prays they would be rooted and established in the love of God. And therefore, that they would somehow come to know the vastness of the unknowable love of God.

He is praying for their spiritual health and wellbeing. And his prayers are bold, asking God to work miraculously in them to produce people who are strong and firm in the faith. Why does he pray this? Because people who are strong in the Lord have joy, peace, endurance, and hope. Paul prays with spiritual eyes. He sees not only their circumstances but their souls. He is living by faith and praying by faith. He is focusing on what is unseen, for that is what matters most because it is eternal. It is what will last.

When we pray for others, we too should remember to pray not only for their external condition but their internal condition as well. And the most urgent thing we can pray for others is for their salvation. Through belief in Jesus, the forgiveness of sins, and salvation, those we love will be safe, happy, and loved for all eternity. It is also urgent to pray for spiritual growth and maturity for loved ones that are already saved.

Our most basic prayer for others is this: God, reveal yourself to them and help them grow in faith and godliness all the days of their lives!

"

> When we pray for others, we too should remember to pray not only for their external condition but their internal condition as well.

daily QUESTIONS

Think of someone you pray for often. List your prayer requests for their life. What physical and spiritual needs do they have?

When you pray for others, do you pray more for their physical needs or spiritual needs? Why is it important to focus on praying for their spiritual needs?

Reread Ephesians 3:14-19. Write down a prayer for someone you love based on Paul's prayer for the Ephesians.

LET'S pray

Let today's Bible reading and study specifically influence your prayers. Avoid reciting the same prayer every day, but bring today's praises and problems to God through this guide.

Our Father: *Refer to the list of attributes on pages 6-7. Write a prayer praising God for who He is in the lives of your loved ones.*

_____
_____
_____
_____
_____

Your Kingdom Come: *Write a prayer expressing your desire for God to build His kingdom and accomplish His will in your life and the world, especially in the lives of those you love.*

_____
_____
_____
_____
_____

Daily Bread: *What are your physical needs today? Write a prayer asking God to meet them, and let Him know you trust Him to meet them. Refer to question 1, and pray for the needs of your loved one as well.*

_____
_____
_____
_____
_____

Forgive Our Sins: *Take a moment to confess, and ask forgiveness for sins you have committed. As you receive God's forgiveness, remember that He has called you to forgive others.*

_____
_____
_____
_____
_____

Deliver Us: *Write a prayer asking God to help you avoid sin and stay close to Him.*

_____
_____
_____
_____
_____
_____

"

Our most basic prayer for others is this: God, reveal yourself to them and help them grow in faith and godliness all the days of their lives!

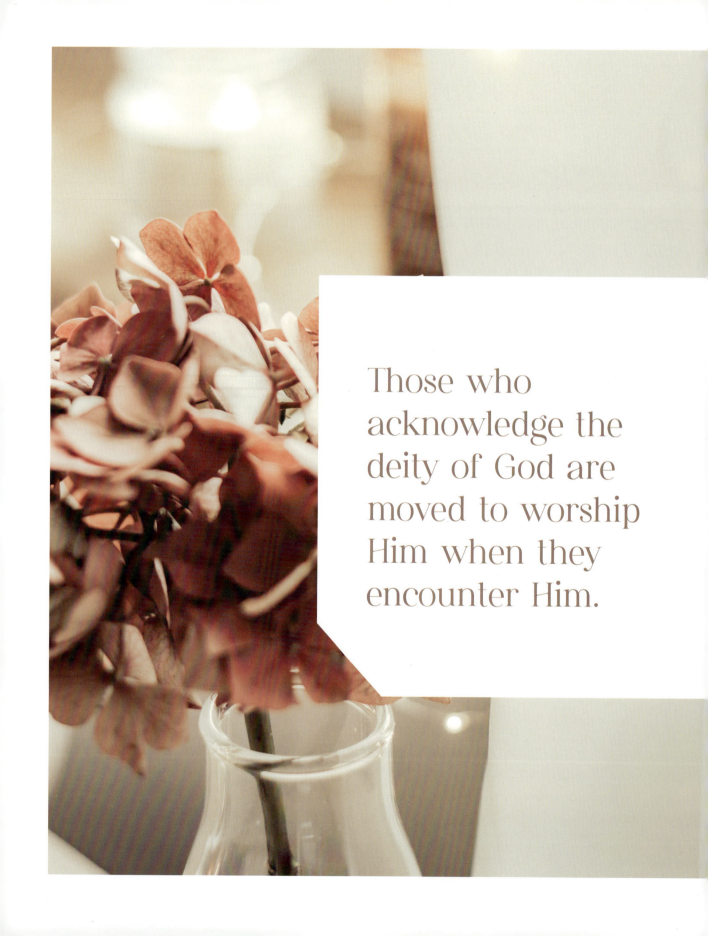

Those who acknowledge the deity of God are moved to worship Him when they encounter Him.

WEEK TWO

day 5

Prayers of Adoration

READ REVELATION 4:8-11, JOHN 4:23-24

Adoration. It is an often overlooked but vitally important part of prayer. Why is it important? Because when we adore God, we put Him in His rightful place in our lives. And when He is in His place as God, we also end up in the right place—as mere men and women. It truly was intentional that Jesus began the Lord's prayer by praising God the Father and ascribing honor to His name. Jesus wants us to do this as well because prayer should be centered on God. Our needs and desires should not be the center of our prayers.

Worship and adoration should be the first words that leave our mouths when we pray. After all, what could be more important to say in the presence of the Lord? Right now, those who are most immediately experiencing the presence of the Lord are in continual worship of Him. They cannot help but exclaim, "Holy, holy, holy, Lord God, the Almighty, who was, who is, and who is to come" (Revelation 4:8) and "our Lord and God, you are worthy to receive glory and honor and power" (Revelation 4:11). Worshiping the Lord when we come to Him in prayer is the most natural response possible. In fact, if we are not moved to worship when we pray, we should ask ourselves why.

If you are just now realizing that it really is not natural for you to praise the Lord in times of prayer, do not feel ashamed. This is the case for all of us at times. But let us learn together how we can overcome this hurdle so that our prayer time begins with genuine worship, leading to true and intimate communion with the Lord.

The Bible gives us some guidance on what may be the cause if we often find ourselves talking to the Lord without first pausing to revere or worship Him. In John 4:24, we learn that true worship happens both in Spirit and in truth.

Worship happens in the innermost parts of us, in ways that cannot be expressed or emoted with our physical being—this is worship in Spirit. As humans, God has breathed His Spirit in us at our creation. And Christians are indwelt by the Holy Spirit at the time of salvation (Galatians 4:6). We are more than flesh and bones. There is a part of us that is spirit. It has been called our heart, our conscience, and many other names. Even those who do not believe in God acknowledge there is a part of us that exists outside of our flesh and bones. If we are not moved to worship God, we may ask ourselves: *Have I brought my whole self into this time of prayer? Or is my outward stance prayer while my inward stance is of worry, stress, and self-reliance?*

Worship also happens in our thoughts and actions—this is worship in truth. While spirit worship happens deep within and is unexplainable as a work of the Holy Spirit within us, worship in truth happens when we pursue and choose to apply the truth of Scripture. To know if we worship God in truth, we could ask ourselves: *Am I pursuing an expanding knowledge of who God is and how He works that will provoke my heart to worship Him? Am I choosing to walk in His ways and honor Him with not just my words but also my actions?*

It should be mentioned that there are times when life is so heavy or hard that to stop and think whether or not we are worshiping God in both spirit and truth before we pray will be impossible. These are the times when all we can manage is to utter, "God, help!" Today's study was meant to be a simple assessment for when we struggle to praise God in times of prayer. It is a helpful tool but not a hard and fast rule. Falling at the feet of the Lord in prayer when our lives are falling apart is in itself a response that exalts the Lord.

Proximity to God, in our knowledge, actions, and inner spirit, creates a natural overflow of praise to God. We see consistently in Scripture that those who acknowledge the deity of God are moved to worship Him when they encounter Him. What do you need to do to move, in spirit or in truth, closer to God in your times of prayer? Today, choose to adore Him when you pray.

> Falling at the feet of the Lord in prayer when our lives are falling apart is in itself a response that exalts the Lord.

daily QUESTIONS

In today's study, we asked ourselves two sets of questions to assess how we are doing in worshiping the Lord in spirit and in truth. Refer to these questions (in italics) on page 80. In which area do you feel you need to grow—worshiping in spirit or worshiping in truth? How can you pursue growth in this area?

When we are not sure what to praise God for, we can look at Scripture. Read Romans 8:31-39, and make a list of all the things God is and does that are worthy of praise in this passage.

We can also find reasons to praise God when we examine our lives. List some ways God has worked in your life below.

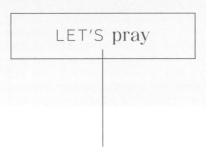

LET'S pray

Let today's Bible reading and study specifically influence your prayers. Avoid reciting the same prayer every day, but bring today's praises and problems to God through this guide.

Our Father: *Refer to the ways God is worthy of praise that you listed in questions 1 and 2. Write a prayer praising God for these things!*

_____
_____
_____
_____

Your Kingdom Come: *Write a prayer expressing your desire for God to build His kingdom and accomplish His will in your life and the world, especially in the lives of those you love.*

_____
_____
_____
_____

Daily Bread: *What are your physical needs today? Write a prayer asking God to meet them.*

_____
_____
_____
_____
_____

Forgive Our Sins: *Take a moment to confess, and ask forgiveness for sins you have committed. As you receive God's forgiveness, remember that He has called you to forgive others.*

_____
_____
_____
_____

Deliver Us: *Write a prayer asking God to help you avoid sin and stay close to Him.*

_____
_____
_____
_____
_____

Today, choose to adore Him when you pray.

Now if any of you lacks wisdom, he should ask God—who gives to all generously and ungrudgingly—and it will be given to him. But let him ask in faith without doubting. For the doubter is like the surging sea, driven and tossed by the wind.

JAMES 1:5-6

weekly REFLECTION

Review all Scripture passages from the week.

Summarize the main points from this week's Scripture readings.

What did you observe from this week's passages about God and His character?

What do this week's passages reveal about the condition of mankind and yourself?

WEEK TWO

How do these passages point to the gospel?

How should you respond to these Scriptures? What specific action steps can you take this week to apply them in your life?

Write a prayer in response to your study of God's Word. Adore God for who He is, confess sins He revealed in your own life, ask Him to empower you to walk in obedience, and pray for anyone who comes to mind as you study.

George Muller's Story

George Muller (1805-1898) may have the most detailed prayer life ever recorded, though he did not start out that way. Although his father wanted him to become a minister, he had no desire for the things of God. As a young man, he found himself a drunk, a liar, and imprisoned on account of his debts. He was convicted over his lifestyle and began reading the Bible to find a way out of his guilt. The Spirit illuminated everything he read, and he understood and received the gift of salvation by faith alone through grace alone.

He began to pastor a small church but refused to take a salary and trusted God for what he needed. He often did not know where his next meal would come from, but God always provided. While pastoring in 1834, he encountered orphaned children in need of a home and felt compelled to help. He prayed that God would provide a way, and He did! Charitable givers supplied everything he needed to open a home with room to house thirty children. Only when the home opened, there were no children for it! Muller realized he had prayed for everything he needed for the home but had not prayed for God to send children in need. He began to pray for children to come. And come they did.

Throughout his almost seventy years of ministering to children, Muller cared for over 10,000 orphans. He ran four orphanages that collectively cared for as many as 2,000 children at once. The needs of the children were overwhelmingly great, but Muller was confident that God could meet each and every one. He was so confident that he committed to never communicate his needs to anyone other than the Lord. He never once asked for help or contributions from others to keep his orphanages funded. And he did not need to, for God supplied every one of his needs. In fact, by the time Muller died, he had recorded over 50,000 answers to specific prayers in his prayer journal. And even more shocking is that 30,000 of these answers arrived on the same day of his prayer!

In his 68th year of ministering to orphans, Muller created a report detailing all that God had provided. He said that to date, God had provided 1,309,627 pounds for his ministry. If Muller lived today, that would be equivalent to over 172,000,000 pounds! Prayer is effective. And God is our ultimate provider. Muller's consistent dependence reveals this to us in an extraordinary way!

> "He often did not know where his next meal would come from, but God always provided."

WEEK THREE

PRAYING THROUGH *the hard stuff*

Sometimes we bow our heads in prayer, and other times life brings us to our knees, and we choose to pray there. We cannot talk about prayer without talking about the hard things because despair, devastation, and desperation are often catalysts to pray.

This week we will talk about praying through anxiety, anger, and sorrow. The keyword is *through*. We cannot pray these emotions away, but we can pray through them. We will also take some time to tread into two tender topics: praying when we have messed up and how to start praying again when we have strayed from it for a while.

Prayer is key to overcoming the physical, emotional, and spiritual difficulties we experience in life. Learning to pray through difficulties will give us passionate and persevering prayer lives.

Jesus Himself shows us how to surrender anxiety and walk in the peace of God through prayer.

WEEK THREE

day 1

Praying Through Anxiety

READ 1 PETER 5:7, MATTHEW 6:27, PHILIPPIANS 4:6-7, LUKE 12:22, MATTHEW 26:36-48

Do not worry about anything (Philippians 4:6). Cast all your cares on Him (1 Peter 5:7). Do not worry about your life (Matthew 6:25). Do these verses sound familiar? Scripture repeatedly tells Christians not to be afraid, fearful, or anxious. Yet anxiety seems to have befriended us all. Fearful thoughts intrude often. And worry is our constant companion. God's commands to "fear not" feel impossible to keep. But they are not! Jesus Himself shows us how to surrender anxiety and walk in the peace of God through prayer.

In Matthew 26:36-48, we see Jesus in pure agony and distress. The Bible says He was sorrowful and troubled. He knew that later that night, He would be betrayed by Judas, arrested, and only days later, He would be crucified and bear the entire weight of God's wrath. Within, He was at war over this. He was anxious.

In His anxiety, Jesus knew exactly where to go. It was not to reason with Judas. It was not to run away from the Pharisees or flee Jerusalem to a place of safety. It was to the Father in prayer. But He did not go to the Father alone. His sorrow was so great that He knew He needed companionship and support. He took Peter, James, and John with Him to pray into the garden of Gethsemane. He left the three disciples in one area of the garden, requesting them to stay awake and keep watch with Him. Then He traveled further into the garden alone.

The Bible says He then fell face down and prayed. He did not kneel or bow in reverence. He crumbled to the ground in agony. With His face to dirt, He prayed, "My Father, if it is possible, let this cup pass from me. Yet not as I will, but as you will" (Matthew 26:39b). It was the cup that was causing Jesus so much anguish. The cup is a common biblical picture used to refer to the wrath of God. We see it in other places like Jeremiah 25:15, which says, "This is what the Lord, the God of Israel, said to me: 'Take this cup of the wine of wrath from my hand and make all the nations to whom I am sending you drink from it.'" When God poured out His wrath in the Old Testament, it was brutal. Men fell by the hundreds. There was disease, famine, and pain. Jesus knew the fullness of God's wrath was soon to be poured on Him and prayed for God to let this cup pass from Him.

Then, He went to check on His friends, who had fallen asleep. He wakes them, pleads with them to stay awake and pray with Him, then goes back to the Father in prayer. He repeats the same prayer, wakes His friends again, then goes back to pray a third time. One moment of prayer was not enough. Jesus enters the Father's presence, asking three total times that He be reprieved of sacrificing His life as a payment for the sins of the world. And when He realizes His closest friends cannot help uphold Him in this moment of despair, He simply walks back into the place of prayer.

After the third time, He prays to the Father from the depths of the garden. Finally, He rises and wakes His disciples and leads them to the place He will be arrested. Jesus entered His time of prayer by falling on His face in anguish. He left it in a much different state, walking assuredly into the plan God had prepared for Him. Even though God's answer to His prayer to be released from death was a "no," He leaves His time of prayer ready to walk in full obedience to the will of the Father.

When we feel anxieties rising and fears overwhelming, may we learn to pray through them like Jesus. In Gethsemane, Jesus gave us an example of how to do this. And He has made a way for all believers to have open, intimate communion with the Father. When anxieties rise, ask for friends to pray with you. Go before the Father in prayer, even if all you can do is fall on your face before Him. And pray again and again until you can release your worries and receive His peace.

> When anxieties rise, ask for friends to pray with you.

daily QUESTIONS

When you experience anxiety, what is your typical response?

Read Jesus's prayers in Matthew 26:39-42. What do you notice about the way He prays through His anxiety? How can you apply this to how you pray when you are anxious?

How might your response to anxiety in your life change this after reading today's study?

LET'S pray

Let today's Bible reading and study specifically influence your prayers. Avoid reciting the same prayer every day, but bring today's praises and problems to God through this guide.

Our Father: What attributes of God (Pages 6-7) do you lean on when you feel anxious? Praise God for how He embodies these attributes.

Your Kingdom Come: Write a prayer expressing your desire for God to build His kingdom and accomplish His will in your life and the world.

Daily Bread: What are your physical needs today? What needs do you feel anxious about? Write a prayer asking God to meet them.

Forgive Our Sins: *Take a moment to confess, and ask forgiveness for sins you have committed. As you receive God's forgiveness, remember that He has called you to forgive others.*

_____
_____
_____
_____
_____

Deliver Us: *Write a prayer asking God to help you avoid sin and stay close to Him.*

_____
_____
_____
_____
_____
_____

"

> Go before the Father in prayer, even if all you can do is fall on your face before Him.

Pride pushes us to anger, but God moves us toward humility.

WEEK THREE

day 2

Praying Through Anger

READ EPHESIANS 4:26-27, GALATIANS 5:20, JAMES 1:19-20, JAMES 4:1-10

Anger. At the first signs of conflict, it begins to bubble within us. We think, *"How could they? This is not fair!"* Usually, we can take a few deep breaths and squelch our displeasure. The problem comes when the conflict persists. The longer we must endure infuriating circumstances, the more our patience wanes. And when we are all out of patience, our red hot anger boils over and often burns those around us. Does the Bible give us a better way to handle anger than to push it down until we explode? Yes, it does.

The Bible has plenty to say about anger. Ephesians 4:26 tells us that anger is not a sin, but we must be careful that it does not lead us to sin. Galatians 5:20 teaches that outbursts of anger are works of the flesh. And James 1:20 encourages us to be quick to listen, slow to speak, and slow to become angry.

But one of the most exhaustive passages on anger is found in James 4:1-10. In these verses, James speaks about the root cause and best cure for anger. Anger stems from the passions and desires that wage war in us. And these are not godly passions but are rooted in selfishness and pride. For example, anger toward one's children is often prideful frustration over their disrespect. But, humility and gentle correction would be the better path. It is just as Galatians 5:19-20 said—that our sinful or fleshly passions lead us to outbursts of anger.

Anger is pride exploding in our thoughts and from our lips. But, in James 4:6, we learn that when the proud humble themselves, God has grace on them. When anger is overtaking our thoughts and emotions, the answer is to draw near to God (James 4:8). And one way to draw near to God is to pray. When we take a step back from our circumstances and take a step toward God, we will begin to realize how sinful our angry outbursts are. We will realize we need cleansing forgiveness, which will move us to repent and ask forgiveness (James 4:8-9). Pride pushes us to anger, but God moves us toward humility. And that is exactly where we should be because it is not the angry and prideful who are honored by God but the humble, lowly, and repentant.

What about times when we are truly experiencing deep injustice, and our anger is righteous? Anger is righteous when we are angry about the same things God is angry about. We should never assume our anger is righteous but should search the Bible to see if our anger aligns with God's. A good place to start if you want to know if your anger is righteous is simply searching for the word "anger" in the Bible. A concordance or online Bible could help with this. Every time the word occurs, take note of what the passage and its larger context tell you about anger. If, in searching Scripture, we find our anger does align with God's, then we must still be careful to not sin in our anger. Anger turns to sin when it is impatient (James 1:20), leads to bitterness, rage, or harsh words (Ephesians 4:31), and when it prevents us from forgiving others (Ephesians 4:32), among other things. To simplify, even being angry over the right things can lead to sin. Righteous anger does not excuse us from submitting to the whole counsel of Scripture.

And we should still pray. God is a God of justice. Romans 12:19 says, "Friends, do not avenge yourselves; instead, leave room for God's wrath, because it is written, 'Vengeance belongs to me; I will repay, says the Lord.'" Submit your anger to the Lord in prayer, knowing that He will act upon it at the right time. This does not necessarily mean we will see the judgment of the Lord, but we can be sure He always acts justly. The psalmists give us wonderful examples of praying through anger. We read in Psalm 25:2, "My God, I trust in you. Do not let me be disgraced; do not let my enemies gloat over me." And Psalm 143:9 says, "Rescue me from my enemies, Lord; I come to you for protection."

Prayer brings our unrighteous anger into the presence of God, where it cannot stay. Prayer also submits our righteous anger to God, trusting that He will bring justice and vengeance fully and completely. Both require humility and drawing near to God. Prayer is one way God wants us to handle anger. Make it your aim to bend your knees when you feel anger rise within you. God will meet you with power in your humility.

> "
> Anger is pride exploding in our thoughts and from our lips.

daily QUESTIONS

When you feel angry, how do you typically handle it?

What does James 4:1-10 teach you about anger? How does this impact the way you deal with anger?

What would it look like for you to submit your anger to the Lord and trust that He will justly avenge and repay?

LET'S pray

Let today's Bible reading and study specifically influence your prayers. Avoid reciting the same prayer every day, but bring today's praises and problems to God through this guide.

Our Father: *Refer to the attributes of God on pages 6-7. Which of these resonates the most with you when you feel anger? Praise God for how He embodies these attributes.*

Your Kingdom Come: *Write a prayer expressing your desire for God to build His kingdom and accomplish His will in your life and the world.*

Daily Bread: *What are your physical needs today? Write a prayer asking God to meet them.*

Forgive Our Sins: *Take a moment to confess, and ask forgiveness for sins you have committed. Take a moment to consider whether you have sinned in your anger, and repent if you have. As you receive God's forgiveness, remember that He has called you to forgive others.*

_____
_____
_____
_____

Deliver Us: *Write a prayer asking God to help you avoid pride and sinful actions when you are angry. Ask God to help you stay close to Him.*

_____
_____
_____
_____

"

God will meet you with power in your humility.

Sin causes guilt, shame, and separation from God.

Praying When You Have Messed Up

READ PSALM 32:3-7, HEBREWS 10:14, COLOSSIANS 2:6

When is it hardest for you to pray? It may be when you are busy or when your mind is easily distracted. But for many, it is when they have messed up, made a mistake. It is when you have been influenced to say and do things that you know are not Christlike. It is when you have stopped prioritizing God, and as a result, you are prioritizing worldly passions and pleasures. It is when you have sinned.

Although it feels good at the moment, and although we are very good at justifying our wrongs, deep down, we know that sin is wrong. We know that it grieves God and often hurts others. *We know.* And it causes us discomfort to admit this. So we choose to avoid dealing with it. And we distance ourselves from the Lord because our mistakes are most glaringly obvious in the presence of His perfection.

Sin causes guilt, shame, and separation from God. And we often believe it is easier to live with the weight of these consequences of sin than to confess. But confession of sin need not scare us. We should be more fearful of the effects of living an unrepentant life. Psalm 32:3-7 describes a life of unconfessed sin as bones wasting away, groaning all day long, and strength dried up. This is a familiar feeling for us all. Sin eats us up from the inside out. Yet, we experience forgiveness, preservation from trouble, and deliverance when we confess it to the Lord. Confession restores our souls.

In the life of a Christian, there is the first confession of sins that leads to salvation (we discuss this further in the Prayer of Salvation extra on page 110), but there should also be an ongoing confession of sins—because Christians still sin. 1 John 1:8-9 tells us that "If we say 'we have no sin,' we are deceiving ourselves and the truth is not in us." No human is free from sin, except Jesus. Therefore, we all must confess our sins.

When a Christian confesses their sin, they are confessing sin that God has already forgiven. The Bible says the one offering of Jesus forgave the sins of believers, and therefore Christians are perfected forever (Hebrews 10:14). Forgiveness for all sins has already been granted to the believer in Christ, but it is still our task to put to death sin in our lives (Colossians 3:5). How do we put sin to death? We begin by admitting its presence in our lives. Then we cry out to God for His assistance to put off our old self, which loves sin, and put on our new self that loves obedience to the Lord.

This is the confession of sins. This is the process through which God helps us grow in godliness. Christians should confess their sins through prayer. In fact, being aware of and confessing sin is a sign of a mature faith. Colossians 2:6-7 says, "So then, just as you have received Christ Jesus as Lord, continue to live in him, being rooted and built up in him and established in the faith, just as you were taught, and overflowing with gratitude." Christians receive the full forgiveness of Christ at salvation, and they continue to walk in Him by confessing their already forgiven sins so that they may be built up and established in the faith.

When we have messed up and sinned against God, we should remind ourselves that all of those sins have been forgiven. Period. And then we should bow before the Lord in prayer, confessing our sins with the knowledge that confession is not weakness but is a means to the growth of our faith.

When Christians make mistakes, they are not condemned. Jesus has paid the debt for all of the sins that will ever be committed. There is no condemnation for those who are in Christ Jesus. But a mark of continued maturity and communion with God is the recognition and confession of sins. Christians should not resist coming to the Father but should run to Him in confession, knowing that in Him they will find relief from guilt and shame, forgiveness, and the grace to overcome temptations to sin in the future (1 Corinthians 10:13).

> There is no condemnation for those who are in Christ Jesus.

daily QUESTIONS

Read 1 John 1:5-10. What do these verses tell you about yourself? What do these verses tell you about God?

In order to confess our sins, we must be aware of them. How can we know when we sin?

Read Colossians 3:1-5. What does it mean to "put to death what belongs to your earthly nature?"

LET'S pray

Let today's Bible reading and study specifically influence your prayers.
Avoid reciting the same prayer every day, but bring today's praises
and problems to God through this guide.

Our Father: *Write a prayer praising God for being gracious toward sinners.*

_____
_____
_____
_____
_____
_____

Your Kingdom Come: *Write a prayer expressing your desire for God to build His kingdom and accomplish His will in your life and the world.*

_____
_____
_____
_____
_____
_____

Daily Bread: *What are your physical needs today? Write a prayer asking God to meet them.*

_____
_____
_____
_____
_____
_____

Forgive Our Sins: *Write a prayer confessing your sins and asking forgiveness for them. Pray through Hebrews 10:14 as you do this. And as you receive God's forgiveness, remember that He has called you to forgive others.*

_____
_____
_____
_____
_____

Deliver Us: *Write a prayer asking God to help you avoid sin and stay close to Him.*

_____
_____
_____
_____
_____
_____
_____

When a Christian confesses their sin, they are confessing sin that God has already forgiven.

The Prayer of Salvation

One of the most talked-about prayers in Christianity is the "prayer of salvation" or the "sinner's prayer." If you have ever been to a church service where the gospel was presented, you have likely heard a pastor tell those who want to be saved from their sin to "repeat this prayer after me." The prayer usually consists of repenting of sins, confessing belief in Christ, and committing to surrender to Christ's leading.

Interestingly, the Bible never actually presents us with a specific prayer that leads to salvation. Instead, Jesus often calls people to believe (John 6:35) and follow Him (Matthew 19:21). And Romans 10:9 teaches, "if you confess with your mouth, 'Jesus is Lord,' and believe in your heart that God raised Him from the dead, you will be saved."

If there was a prayer formula that led to salvation, Scripture would clearly demonstrate it. But this is not the case. Instead, Scripture demonstrates that salvation is an issue of the heart. It is not the words you say but the belief in your heart that leads to salvation. Salvation is the work of God in response to one's faith in Christ.

However, a natural overflow of believing in God is praying to Him. And it is important to pray to Him the moment you realize the depth of your sin and your need for a Savior. This is where the tradition of the prayer of salvation comes from. It is meant to be a sincere conversation between a repentant sinner and a gracious God, not just simply speaking the words without a heart desire for change.

If you have not yet entered into a saving relationship with Jesus, you can pray a prayer of salvation today. There is nothing magical about these words. They are simply communicating your admission of your sin and your belief in God's saving power. Salvation is an issue of the heart.

Your prayer could go something like this:

God, I've sinned against You, and I know that I can never make this right on my own. I trust that Jesus's sacrifice was enough to bring me into a real, life-changing relationship with You. Redeem my life, Lord. I cannot do it apart from You. I am making the choice to walk with You in my mind, heart, and actions everyday, and I want to start today. Amen.

Christ suffered and died so that others might find life through His death.

WEEK THREE

day 4

Praying Through Sorrow

READ ISAIAH 53, PSALM 42

Sorrow. It is an emotion that often looms in our minds and hearts, yet we seldom know what to do with it when it arrives. Shall we shove it off to the side and tell it to be joyful in all things? Shall we hide it for fear that exposing it will be a burden to those around us? Shall we ignore it altogether and tell ourselves things are fine, even when they clearly are not?

Scripture gives us a better way to handle sadness and sorrow. We can lament. Lament is a biblical way to work through sadness. We see lament throughout the Bible, most notably in the books of Lamentations and Psalms. Specifically, the psalms teach us how to lament through prayer. Each psalm was written as a song you can sing to the Lord corporately or privately if you prefer. These songs teach us how to pray. And remarkably, almost half of the songs contain expressions of grief, despair, and sadness—that is to say, almost half of them contain lament.

The people who wrote the psalms are referred to as psalmists. We know the identity of some of the psalmists, and others we do not. King David wrote about half of the psalms, and we know a lot about his life because it is detailed in 1 and 2 Kings and 1 and 2 Chronicles. David made many mistakes that caused him much grief. He also experienced great turmoil when the king who preceded him, Saul, wanted to kill him. He certainly had reasons to be sorrowful. He also knew that pain and sorrow should not be swept away, but rather, they should be embraced. They knew that to come out of their sadness, they needed to work through it. It would do us well to learn from their example. Our sorrow needs a place to be vented and released, too.

The psalms of lament all follow a similar arc, and this informs how our prayers of sorrow can look. First, prayers of lament are honest expressions of sorrow toward the Lord. Then, they ask God to intervene in the agony. Finally, they hope in God as the One who can relieve distress. We will look at each of these parts of a prayer of lament more closely.

Prayers of lament are honest expressions of sorrow toward the Lord. Even if we can barely utter the words, even if we blame God, or question His plan, we do well to bring our profound pain to Him in prayer. The psalmists often said things we rarely ever speak aloud. Consider these psalms: "My tears have been my food day and night" (Psalm 42:3), "I am deeply depressed" (Psalm 42:6), and "I will say to God, my rock, 'Why have you forgotten me?'" (Psalm 42:9).

Prayers of lament do not need to be filtered. When you pray, bringing your sorrows to the Lord, you can come to Him just as you are. But praying in agony is only the first step. Next, we should pray for God's intervention in our distressing situation. We see this in the following verses: "Vindicate me, God" (Psalm 43:1) and "Send your light and your truth; let them lead me" (Psalm 43:3).

Bringing our sorrow before the Lord has a purpose. The Lord can help us in our distress, spiritually and physically. He may grant us reprieve from our situation, or He may simply give us His strength to endure, but He always answers our tear-soaked prayers. And that is why prayers of lament end with hope in the Lord. Both Psalm 42 and 43 display this:

> Why, my soul, are you so dejected?
> Why are you in such turmoil?
> Put your hope in God, for I will still praise him,
> my Savior and my God. (Psalm 42:5)

> Then I will come to the altar of God,
> to God, my greatest joy.
> I will praise you with the lyre,
> God, my God. (Psalm 43:4)

Your prayers of lament can be messy and teary, but do not forget to conclude them by remembering the faithfulness of God. In the direst of circumstances, God is present. Jesus Himself showed us this because He, too, was a man of sorrows. In fact, Isaiah 53:3 tells us that he was well acquainted with grief (ESV).

Yet, His sorrow was not proof that God did not love Him. Rather, the sorrow was proof that God used His pain in order to show His love to the world. Isaiah 53:11 says that the anguish of Christ's soul led to many being counted as righteous. Christ suffered and died so that others might find life through His death. Sorrow in the hands of the Lord has a purpose. God used Jesus's pain to pardon the sins of all who believe in Him. And He uses our pain for a purpose, too. We may never know what it is on this side of heaven, but we can still trust that He has a good purpose for it.

When we experience deep sorrow, let us bring it to the Lord. Let us cry and groan before the Lord rather than avoid and bury our pain within ourselves. Let us ask God to intercede, and let us trust in the hope that He offers us. It is good to lament. And God is good in our times of lamenting. We can be sure of this!

In the direst of circumstances, God is present.

daily QUESTIONS

What is causing sorrow in your life right now? Write out an honest expression of your sorrow to the Lord.

Refer to Psalm 42 and Isaiah 53. How does God intervene in times of sorrow?

Refer to the attributes of God on pages 6-7. What specific attributes of God help us place our hope in Him, even when we are in times of great sorrow?

LET'S pray

Let today's Bible reading and study specifically influence your prayers. Avoid reciting the same prayer every day, but bring today's praises and problems to God through this guide.

Our Father: Write a prayer praising God for how He embodies the attributes you listed in question 3.

_____
_____
_____
_____
_____

Your Kingdom Come: Write a prayer expressing your desire for God to build His kingdom and accomplish His will in your life and the world. Lift your sorrows to Him, and ask Him to use them as part of His redemptive plan for the world.

_____
_____
_____
_____

Daily Bread: What are your physical needs today? Do you need God to intervene in your sorrow? Write a prayer asking God to do just that.

_____
_____
_____
_____
_____

Forgive Our Sins: *Take a moment to confess, and ask forgiveness for sins you have committed. As you receive God's forgiveness, remember that He has called you to forgive others.*

_____
_____
_____
_____
_____

Deliver Us: *Write a prayer asking God to help you avoid sin and stay close to Him.*

_____
_____
_____
_____
_____
_____
_____

> Prayers of lament are honest expressions of sorrow toward the Lord.

Separation.
This is the barrier
to prayer.

WEEK THREE

day 5

The Open Invitation to Pray Again

READ EXODUS 40:34, HEBREWS 4:14-5:10, MATTHEW 27:51, ROMANS 8:31-34, HEBREWS 10:11-18

This day's study was written for the one who has taken an intentional or unintentional break from prayer. It is for the one who has felt guilt heaped upon them when they consider where their prayer life could be and where it is. To this person is extended a grace-filled, long-suffering, and open-armed invitation to pray again.

In the beginning, God created a paradise garden and then placed man in it. He gave man a job—to rule over the earth and subdue the animals in it. He gave him a helper—woman. And He walked in the garden with man, freely communicating with him. This communication is God's intended design for communion with people. This is what He intends for His relationship with you.

But man could not keep the rules of the garden. Instead, he believed he knew better than God, and he went against God's design. He sinned. As a result, perfect communion with God was broken. Man was banished from the paradise and separated from God's presence.

Separation. This is the barrier to prayer. We are separated from God. Our busy lives, distracted hearts, and mixed up priorities keep us apart from God.

In the Old Testament, God made a way for people to come close to Him. He set a standard and required shed blood to pay (or atone) for times the standard was not met. He had the wandering Israelites build Him a tabernacle so he could have a dwelling place among them. But only the high priest was allowed to enter the most holy place at the center of the tabernacle where God dwelled. Only the one man, when fully atoned for, cleansed, and purified might enter His presence. With sacrifices in their hands, the rest waited outside to pay for their sins and guilt, but their feet never entered His presence.

Then, Jesus came. Jesus is the Great High Priest. The human high priests offered sacrifices in the Old Testament to atone for sins one at a time, but Jesus offered himself as a sacrifice to atone for all sins for all time when He died on the cross. He gave His life to pay for all sins. He gave His all for all sinners.

And when He did this, the veil tore in two. The veil was the piece of fabric that was placed around the most holy place where God's presence dwelled inside the temple. That veil separated God from sinners, and Jesus's death caused it to split wide open—God and man, no longer separated, but God dwelling in and among the ones whom the Great High Priest had atoned.

Therefore, let us not erect another veil. Let us not hang a veil of guilt where God has not hung one. Let us not hang the veil of sin where God has not. Let us not hang the veil of unworthiness or unacceptance or fear where God has not.

There is now no condemnation nor separation for those who are in Christ Jesus. Through the forgiveness of Jesus, we find a gracious invitation to pray, to come boldly before the High Priest who has already paid the price and spilt the blood required. So, just come. Come after you have had a season of neglecting prayer. Come after you forgot. Come after you chose to wander for a while. Just come.

"

> Jesus offered himself as a sacrifice to atone for all sins for all time when He died on the cross.

daily QUESTIONS

How do you feel when you are in a time of struggling to be consistent in prayer? Embarrassed? Reluctant? Indifferent?

What does it mean to you that Jesus is your Great High Priest?

What are the benefits of God ending the separation between Himself and you?

LET'S pray

Let today's Bible reading and study specifically influence your prayers. Avoid reciting the same prayer every day, but bring today's praises and problems to God through this guide.

Our Father: *Write a prayer praising God for being patient with your sin and weaknesses.*

_____
_____
_____
_____
_____

Your Kingdom Come: *Write a prayer expressing your desire for God to build His kingdom and accomplish His will in your life and the world.*

_____
_____
_____
_____
_____

Daily Bread: *What are your physical needs today? Write a prayer asking God to do just that.*

_____
_____
_____
_____
_____

Forgive Our Sins: *Take a moment to confess, and ask forgiveness for sins you have committed. Praise Him that through Jesus, all of your sins are completely forgiven. As you receive God's forgiveness, remember that He has called you to forgive others.*

_____

_____

_____

_____

Deliver Us: *Write a prayer asking God to help you avoid sin, including the sin of not prioritizing your relationship with Him. Ask Him to help you stay close to Him.*

_____

_____

_____

_____

"

> There is now no condemnation nor separation for those who are in Christ Jesus.

WEEK THREE
Scripture Memory

Don't worry about anything, but in everything, through prayer and petition with thanksgiving, present your requests to God. And the peace of God, which surpasses all understanding, will guard your hearts and minds in Christ Jesus.

PHILIPPIANS 4:6-7

weekly REFLECTION

Review all Scripture passages from the week.

Summarize the main points from this week's Scripture readings.

What did you observe from this week's passages about God and His character?

What do this week's passages reveal about the condition of mankind and yourself?

WEEK THREE

How do these passages point to the gospel?

How should you respond to these Scriptures? What specific action steps can you take this week to apply them in your life?

Write a prayer in response to your study of God's Word. Adore God for who He is, confess sins He revealed in your own life, ask Him to empower you to walk in obedience, and pray for anyone who comes to mind as you study.

Susanna Wesley's Story

Susanna Wesley was the wife of an English preacher, Samuel Wesley, and the mother of nineteen children. She lived from 1669-1742, and in her 72 years, she saw more pain and heartache than almost seems possible. Nine of her children died, most of those in infancy, some by natural causes and others by terrible accidents. Her home was burnt to the ground twice, and one of those times by her own church members who disapproved of her husband's Sunday sermons. Her husband deserted her once for several months when the couple disagreed on a political matter. And yet another time, he was thrown in jail for five months because he owed a great debt that he could not pay due to his poor financial management.

Yet, in all of this, Susanna clung tightly to the Lord and continued to diligently raise her children to love and fear God. She wrote an entire curriculum of theology and doctrine, which she taught each of her children from a young age. She knew it was her responsibility as their mother to lead them in the ways of God, and even under dire circumstances, she never wavered from this commitment.

But what is maybe most extraordinary about Susanna is her prayer life. When she was young, she promised to give the Lord two hours in prayer for every one hour she spent idly. Once she had a house full of children who needed tending, she found this almost impossible, so she settled for giving the Lord two hours per day in prayer. In order to accomplish this, when it was time for her to pray, she would sit in a rocking chair and drape an apron over her head. When the apron was atop her head, everyone knew it was her time of prayer, and she was not to be interrupted.

What did she pray for during those two hours? We know from letters she penned that she prayed for her husband, her children, and the members of her church. In a letter to one of her sons, she expressed that her prayers for her children often ended with tears rolling down her cheeks as she begged God to draw them to

Him. She desperately wanted her children to find salvation in Jesus and live lives dedicated to God. And as far as we can tell, God granted her this desire.

In fact, two of her sons, John and Charles, went on to reach millions of people with the gospel of Jesus Christ in their lifetimes and beyond. John is said to have preached as many as 40,000 sermons in his life, and by his words and works, the Methodist denomination was founded, which today has upwards of 3 million members. Hours and hours of prayers. Millions reached for Christ.

There have been, no doubt, countless souls who have come to know Christ because of the prayers of Susanna Wesley and the way God answered them in John and Charles.

Perhaps Susanna could have thought of a more immediately productive way to spend those two hours a day, but her prayers have produced eternal results that she likely could never have fathomed. No minute spent praying is wasted. We may not see the fruit of our prayers in our lifetime, but let that never deter us from praying anyway.

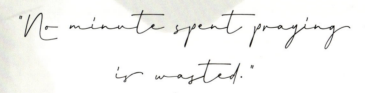

"No minute spent praying is wasted."

WEEK FOUR

MAKING PRAYER
a practice

If your prayer life was dim when you began this study, like the slow dulling of once-lit embers, then hopefully, learning of the beauty, wonder, and mystery of prayer over the past three weeks has set it ablaze. But like any blazing fire, it will not stay lit unless you consistently tend to it.

This week we will learn how to make a prayer a habit. We will cover everything from establishing a rhythm of prayer in your life to how to come back to practicing prayer when you have taken an intentional or unintentional break.

As you establish your prayer rhythm this week, do not focus on being a perfectly prayerful person. Focus on making prayer and the presence of God a priority in your life. Practicing prayer is as much about adjusting your heart as it is about adjusting your schedule.

If you shift your heart to prioritize prayer and practice the rhythms, we will discuss, this could be the beginning of a lifetime of powerful, passionate, disciplined prayer. Now, let us get started making prayer a practice!

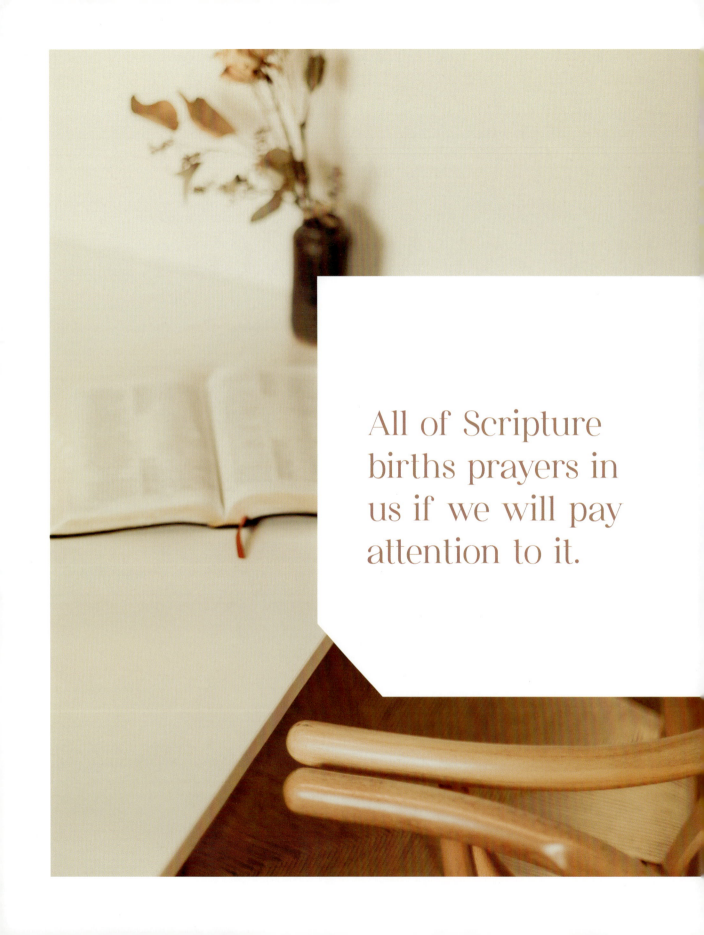

All of Scripture births prayers in us if we will pay attention to it.

WEEK FOUR
day 1

Praying Scripture

READ 2 TIMOTHY 3:16-17

Prayer should not be mundane and repetitive. But sometimes it is! We can get stuck repeating familiar phrases and the same old prayer requests time after time after time. It can start to feel more like a monotonous chore than speaking to the Creator of the world. Have you experienced this?

There is a very practical solution to this problem, and believe it or not, you have already been practicing it throughout this study. If you want to get out of a humdrum prayer rut, pray Scripture! When searching for lively and impassioned words to say to God, we need look no further than God's Word. When we pray God's Word, we avoid praying prayers centered on our thoughts, and we pray prayers centered on God's thoughts. While God always invites us to share our thoughts with Him, He no doubt also wants us to center our hearts on His thoughts as well.

Scripture expands our prayer language by showing us how other believers in Christ who have walked through life's ups and downs communicated with God. Jesus Himself also teaches us how to pray in Scripture. This is the exact reason we have been praying using the Lord's Prayer model each day of this study. Scripture-based prayer is a prayer that is shaped by God's very words!

How do we pray Scripture? We pray Scripture by reading and interpreting the Scripture correctly, then praying the exact words of their intended meaning as a prayer to God. To further explain this process, we will walk through these two steps with a familiar Bible passage.

2 Timothy 3:16-17 reads, "All Scripture is inspired by God and is profitable for teaching, for rebuking, for correcting, for training in righteousness, so that the man of God may be complete, equipped for every good work." After careful

study of this text, we would find that the intended meaning of this passage is to express the divine authority and total sufficiency of Scripture in the life of the believer. This means the Bible is the very Word of God—His very own words, sufficient to instruct believers in all matters that arise in life.

Based on these two truths, the words of the Bible equip His people for all the things—great and small—God calls them to do. What an incredible truth! Now, we will pray this truth. Our prayer could go something like this:

Father, thank You for so graciously giving us Your word. Whenever I face a difficult situation, need wisdom, or have a question about faith, I know that I have the Bible to inform and instruct me. And I am so comforted by that! Every time I read or hear Your word, Lord, please soften my heart to hear how it might teach, rebuke, correct, and train me in righteousness. I want to live rightly! Help me to hear how to do that when I read Your words. And Lord, I know that You have prepared for me good works and that You will equip me for them as the Bible trains me in righteousness. Make my heart receptive to Your words that I may be fully equipped for everything You have called me to do. Teach me to love and cherish Your word more than I ever have before. It is my lifeline and my lamp. Thank You, Lord, for the precious gift of the Bible. Amen.

The beauty of praying Scripture is that the Bible is vast, and there are thousands upon thousands of prayers inside of it just waiting for you to discover and use them as prayers. In fact, prayer is often the most natural reaction to Bible reading.

The Psalms make our hearts cry out for truth and justice alongside the oppressed psalmists. The Gospels draw us near to the tender heart of Jesus and encourage us to whisper our needs to Him. The Epistles convict and lead us to pray prayers of repentance. The wisdom books make us humbly ask for God's wisdom to reside in us like it did in Solomon. All of Scripture births prayers in us if we will pay attention to it.

Part of making prayer a habit is praying Scripture regularly. As often as you read the Bible, pray the Bible.

"

Scripture-based prayer is a prayer that is shaped by God's very words!

daily QUESTIONS

Read Psalm 23. What does this psalm tell you about who God is?

Read Romans 3:23-24. What do these verses tell you about the sinfulness of man and the gift of salvation in Christ?

Read Romans 12:1-2. What do these verses tell you about how God wants believers in Jesus to live their lives?

LET'S pray

Let today's Bible reading and study specifically influence your prayers.
Avoid reciting the same prayer every day, but bring today's praises
and problems to God through this guide.

Our Father: *Refer to your answer to question 1. Write a prayer using Psalm 23 to praise God for who He is.*

_____
_____
_____
_____
_____

Your Kingdom Come: *Write a prayer expressing your desire for God to build His kingdom and accomplish His will in your life and the world.*

_____
_____
_____
_____
_____

Daily Bread: *What are your physical needs today? Write a prayer asking God to do just that.*

_____
_____
_____
_____
_____

Forgive Our Sins: *Refer to your answer to question 2. Write a prayer using Romans 3:23-24 to confess, and ask forgiveness for sins you have committed. As you receive God's forgiveness, remember that He has called you to forgive others.*

_____
_____
_____
_____

Deliver Us: *Refer to your answer to question 3. Write a prayer using Romans 12:1-2 to ask God to help you avoid sin and stay close to Him.*

_____
_____
_____
_____

"

> Part of making prayer a habit is praying Scripture regularly. As often as you read the Bible, pray the Bible.

We should pray on purpose.

WEEK FOUR
day 2

The Place of Prayer

READ LUKE 5:1-16, MARK 6:46, LUKE 4:42, LUKE 6:12, MATTHEW 14:23, JOHN 11:54

From time to time, we may think things like:

I am too busy to sit down and pray, so I just pray a little here and there throughout my day.
I will start spending more time in prayer as soon as life slows down.
Every time I try to spend time in prayer, I am interrupted. So why even try?

The average pace of life for many of us is furious and frenzied. We are the keepers of people, schedules, homes, and careers. We juggle a lot, and as a result, our calendars are crammed full. This leaves little time for prayer, so we tend to shove it in the cracks of our days when we are going through something hard and forgo it all together when things are going just fine.

When our days are full of everything but prayer, it might seem like we have a busyness problem, but ultimately we have a priority problem. And Jesus shows us how to fix it. Consider the life of Jesus. Do you think there has ever been a person who was more in-demand? The Gospels tell of massive crowds following Him from place to place, countless souls that thirsted for the hope and healing He offered, and many who simply showed up for the free food and displays of power. The demands on our lives are minuscule compared to the ones placed on His.

And do you ever think there has been a person with a more pressing schedule or a more important mission than Jesus? To show the world what God is like, defeat sin and death, and commission the start of the Church seems like the paramount life mission.

We can learn from Jesus's high-demand, high-pressure life how we ought to treat prayer in our own fast-paced lives. Even with people always pressing in and the weight of the world on His shoulders, Jesus was not frenzied. He was focused.

Over and over again, we see Jesus sneaking away from crowds, rising early, staying up late, and slipping away from the demands of others to go to a desolate place and pray to His Father.

Luke 5:1-16 provides a perfect picture of Jesus prioritizing the place of prayer. The chapter opens with a crowd that has gathered around Jesus to hear Him teach. Jesus teaches the crowd from a boat. Then He invites the fisherman aboard the boat to become His first disciples after providing them with a miraculous catch of fish. Afterward, He heals a leper in a nearby town, which astounds everyone.

Jesus's fame was increasing by the minute. Many came to see the man who was God. But instead of capitalizing on the moment or spending every waking hour serving and healing those in need, Jesus prioritized time spent in prayer to His Father. He left the people and went to hidden and lonely places to pray.

We do not have detailed descriptions of Jesus's prayer time, but we do have glimpses of what He prayed about during His times alone with God. We know He sought the Father's will and that He submitted His own will (Matthew 26:39). We know that He likely prayed in accordance with the Lord's Prayer because that is how He instructed the disciples to pray (Matthew 6:9-13). We know that He used prayer and time with the Father to recharge and rest (Luke 5:16). Prayer orders our lives, inside and out. Jesus knew that. How would our lives change if we also believed this?

What an effort it must have been for Jesus to arise early, sneak past the clamoring crowds, and walk far enough that He found Himself alone with God. He was setting an example for us. While we want to believe that busyness is a valid excuse to not show up at a specific time and place to pray, it is not. Jesus's example is clear. Make the time. Find the place. Focused and intentional prayer must be a priority. We should pray on purpose.

"

> Focused and intentional prayer must be a priority.

daily QUESTIONS

How would your schedule change if you chose to prioritize times of prayer?

Choose a time when you will commit to pray. When is it? How long is it?

Choose a place where you will commit to pray. Where is it?

How will you handle disruptions to your prayer time?

LET'S pray

Let today's Bible reading and study specifically influence your prayers. Avoid reciting the same prayer every day, but bring today's praises and problems to God through this guide.

Our Father: *Write a prayer praising God for who He is. Refer to the attributes of God on pages 6-7 if needed.*

_____
_____
_____
_____
_____

Your Kingdom Come: *Write a prayer expressing your desire for God to build His kingdom and accomplish His will in your life and the world. Ask God to help you prioritize time to pray as that is one means through which He accomplishes His will in the world.*

_____
_____
_____
_____
_____

Daily Bread: *What are your physical needs today? Write a prayer asking God to do just that.*

_____
_____
_____
_____
_____

Forgive Our Sins: *Take a moment to confess, and ask forgiveness for sins you have committed. As you receive God's forgiveness, remember that He has called you to forgive others.*

_____
_____
_____
_____

Deliver Us: *Refer to your answer to question 3. Write a prayer using Romans 12:1-2 to ask God to help you avoid sin and stay close to Him.*

_____
_____
_____
_____

"

Jesus's example is clear.
Make the time. Find the place.

Perfect prayer is not your goal; growth in prayer is.

WEEK FOUR

day 3

The Time to Pray

READ COLOSSIANS 4:2, 1 THESSALONIANS 5:17, ROMANS 12:12, HEBREWS 4:12

Yesterday we talked about the challenging but necessary task of spending dedicated time in prayer. Today, we are going to speak even more practically about how we can do this.

The Bible gives us the charge in 1 Thessalonians 5:17 to pray constantly. Constantly? When we struggle to find five minutes to focus on prayer, a command to pray constantly can feel downright impossible to fulfill. When Paul gave this instruction to the Christians at Thessalonica, he was painting a word picture of continual communion with God, not giving a rigid command. The Greek word used in the original text for "constantly" was *adialeiptōs*. It was a word often used to describe a hacking cough. That is not exactly a pleasant analogy for constant prayer, but it is an effective one. A persistent cough hangs around no matter what else you are doing. It starts with a tickle in your throat that eventually must be addressed with a forceful cough.

The type of continual prayer we are called to take part in is similar. It does not consume our every waking moment. We surely need to focus on other things at times. But it is an active part of every phase of our day. And if we pay attention to it, we will probably feel a nudge in the depths of our hearts from the Holy Spirit to stop and pray.

Praying constantly could be described as being aware of and sensitive to God and His will in all of the big and small moments of daily life. It is being aware that you are always in the presence of God because He is omnipresent. It is knowing that you have continual access to God and can call out to Him for help at any moment. And it is believing that His Holy Spirit resides in you and may speak, convict, or direct you at any moment. Praying constantly is being aware of God and having the ears of your heart bent in His direction.

So how does this lead us to a practical practice of prayer? Well, practically speaking, if we want to work toward constant prayer, we can look for the times in our day when we are least aware of the presence of God and make a concerted effort to stop and pray there. Maybe you tend to forget about God as you scurry from task to task at work. Maybe you have a hard time hearing God's voice as the whines and cries of your children escalate throughout the day. Or maybe you tune God out in the evening when you lean back on the couch and turn on the television.

Whenever you are most likely to be tuned in to your inner thoughts or outer commotion rather than the presence of the Lord, make it a practice to pray daily in those moments.

You may find the best way to continually refocus your attention on the Lord is to pray during the natural breaks in your day. A break in your day may come when commuting to work or sitting in the carpool pickup line after school. It may be at meals or at bedtime. Taking time to stop and remember God during these natural breaks in your day will center your heart before going on to your next task.

The goal of the time we spend praying is not to check the "pray continuously" box but rather, to continually submit our plans and will to the Lord's while asking for His provision for the task at hand. It is simply to commune seamlessly with God throughout your day.

The answer to when we should pray is that we should pray *always*. Do not let this high standard intimidate you. We will spend our whole lives growing in the practice of prayer. The only person who prayed perfectly was Jesus. Perfect prayer is not your goal; growth in prayer is.

As we end today's study, remember that Jesus sympathizes with our weaknesses in all areas, including prayer, and invites us to freely ask Him for the help we need to do what He has called us to do (Hebrews 4:16).

"

Praying constantly is being aware of God and having the ears of your heart bent in His direction.

daily QUESTIONS

At what points in your day are you least aware of God's presence?

What natural breaks in your day could be a time of prayer and reconnection to God?

How can you make it a priority to connect with God at the times you listed above? Can you use a physical or digital reminder to remind you to pray?

LET'S pray

Let today's Bible reading and study specifically influence your prayers. Avoid reciting the same prayer every day, but bring today's praises and problems to God through this guide.

Our Father: Write a prayer praising God for who He is. Refer to the attributes of God on pages 6-7 if needed.

_____
_____
_____
_____
_____

Your Kingdom Come: Write a prayer expressing your desire for God to build His kingdom and accomplish His will in your life and the world. Ask God to help you prioritize time to pray as that is one means through which He accomplishes His will in the world.

_____
_____
_____
_____
_____

Daily Bread: What are your physical needs today? Write a prayer asking God to do just that.

_____
_____
_____
_____
_____

Forgive Our Sins: *Take a moment to confess, and ask forgiveness for sins you have committed. As you receive God's forgiveness, remember that He has called you to forgive others.*

_____
_____
_____
_____

Deliver Us: *Write a prayer asking God to help you avoid sin and stay close to Him.*

_____
_____
_____
_____
_____
_____

Praying constantly could be described as being aware of and sensitive to God and His will in all of the big and small moments of daily life.

> Prayer certainly is not only a private activity but also a communal one.

WEEK FOUR
day 4

Praying in Community

READ GALATIANS 6:2, ROMANS 12:5, LUKE 9:28, MATTHEW 6:5-8, JAMES 5:13-18

Is there anything more intimidating than being called upon to pray in front of others? Whether it is a prayer before a family meal or a prayer to begin a small group meeting, many of us feel afraid to pray aloud.

There is nothing wrong with feeling apprehensive about praying around others. However, all too often, this apprehension leads us to not pray with others at all. God certainly intends for us to pray alone sometimes but definitely not all of the time. When we pray together, we fulfill many of God's commands for the body of Christ. We carry one another's burdens (Galatians 6:2), enter into the pains and joys of others (Romans 12:15), live in unity, and spur one another on toward love and good works (Hebrews 10:24).

For as many times as Jesus went off alone to pray, He also had times when He prayed with others. In Luke 9:28-36, Jesus invites Peter, James, and John to come away and pray with Him. In Matthew 26:36-46, Jesus took the same three with Him into His most intense and personal prayer time ever recorded in the garden of Gethsemane. And it was when the disciples were with Jesus praying in Luke 11:1-4 that they asked Him to teach them to pray, and He gave them the Lord's Prayer. Jesus even begins the Lord's Prayer with "*Our* Father," not "*my* Father," which suggests prayer should be done corporately. Prayer certainly is not only a private activity but also a communal one.

We see this not only in the life of Jesus but also in the early Church in Acts and the Epistles. Acts 2:42 says they, the church community, devoted themselves to prayer. For example, they prayed together for boldness in the face of persecution, and God answered by filling them with His Spirit and the fortitude to continue to speak the word of God (Acts 4:31).

They prayed fervently for Peter to be released from prison (Acts 12:5), and an angel of the Lord miraculously freed him soon after (Acts 12:6-11). Corporate prayer for the will of God to prevail and for the needs of the people to be met was a common occurrence in the early church. It is a less common occurrence in our modern-day churches that sometimes sacrifice corporate prayer to keep up with the hurried, impersonal, and individualistic lives most of us lead. But the practice of corporate prayer is too important to dismiss because we are too busy or too embarrassed. Because the Bible gives us such solid reason to believe we were meant to pray together, the rest of today's study will focus on how we can practically live a life that prioritizes communal prayer with others.

First, we can choose to pray as soon as a prayer request is made. It is not a rare occurrence for people to ask for prayer. Whether through a text or in passing in the church lobby or on the sidelines of a children's soccer game, people will ask that we pray for things near and dear to them. And generally, we respond with, "I will be praying!" But what if instead, we responded with, "Can I pray for you right now?" In this way, we prioritize not only praying for one another but praying with one another.

Second, we can prioritize asking for prayer from our brothers and sisters in Christ. There is no such thing as "pulling yourself up by your bootstraps" in Christianity. There are no bonus points for handling all of your ails and trials on your own. Instead, we are to carry one another's burdens (Galatians 6:2) and readily enter into the pains and joys of others (Romans 12:15). When we ask for others to pray for us when we need prayer, we give them the chance to fulfill God's commission for all believers to live in unity and spur one another toward love and good works (Hebrews 10:24).

And third, we can push past fear and embrace communal prayer by remembering that prayer is not for show before man but for petition before God (Matthew 6:5-8). The words you say aloud in prayer are not meant for earthly ears but for God's heavenly hearing. This should be a relief! Your prayers do not need to sound eloquent, and they do not need to be long. You can just say what needs to be said to a God who already knows but who delights to hear your voice make these requests all the same. The pressure is off. You can simply pray.

When we believe in Jesus and are saved, we enter into a relationship with God and join a family of brothers and sisters in Christ. Prayer is vital to our relationship with God, and we must pray with and for our Christian family members. Corporate prayer is a bright and vibrant thread in the prayer tapestry God intends to weave in our lives. If we avoid it or exclude it, we will be missing a part of prayer that Jesus demonstrated for us—one that God has commanded from us.

> Prayer is vital to our relationship with God, and we must pray with and for our Christian family members.

daily QUESTIONS

Think about your corporate prayer life. Do you prioritize praying with others? Why or why not?

Which one of the three practical tips for prioritizing corporate prayer stood out to you? How can you include this in your life this week?

Reach out to a friend, and ask them to pray for a need you currently have.

Day 4 / 153

LET'S pray

Let today's Bible reading and study specifically influence your prayers. Avoid reciting the same prayer every day, but bring today's praises and problems to God through this guide.

Our Father: Write a prayer praising God for who He is. Refer to the attributes of God on pages 6-7 if needed.

_____
_____
_____
_____
_____

Your Kingdom Come: Write a prayer expressing your desire for God to build His kingdom and accomplish His will in your life and the world.

_____
_____
_____
_____
_____

Daily Bread: What are your physical needs today? Write a prayer asking God to fulfill those needs. Ask a friend if you can pray for their needs today as well.

_____
_____
_____
_____
_____

Forgive Our Sins: *Take a moment to confess, and ask forgiveness for sins you have committed. As you receive God's forgiveness, remember that He has called you to forgive others.*

_____
_____
_____
_____
_____

Deliver Us: *Write a prayer asking God to help you avoid sin and stay close to Him.*

_____
_____
_____
_____
_____

"

> Corporate prayer is a bright and vibrant thread in the prayer tapestry God intends to weave in our lives.

Our prayer may be as simple as, "Lord, help me want to pray!"

WEEK FOUR

day 5

Praying When You Don't Feel Like It

READ HEBREWS 12:7-13, HEBREWS 4:14-16, JOHN 14:25-27, HEBREWS 3:7-13, PSALM 51

We can be honest with each other, right? And honestly? There are times when we know we should pray, know how to pray, and know that God hears our prayers, but we still simply do not want to pray.

Emotions and desires are fickle that way. They stray easily and change courses often. How should we handle these moments? When prayer is not our desire, we should strive to make it our discipline. Making prayer our discipline means we practice it because it is good and right, even when we would rather not. We act according to what we know is true rather than how we feel.

Discipline is not usually fun or enjoyable. Just ask a toddler who has been told "no." They will likely let you know at the loudest decibel available to them that doing what is right instead of what they want is not all it is cracked up to be—at least in the moment. But ask that same toddler, once they have grown into a young adult, how they feel about their parents' steady guidance and correction, and they will have a drastically different answer. They will be thankful for it. It was better to learn self-control at age 4 so that at age 24 they can say "no" to impulsive purchases and stay out of debt. It was better to learn to calmly communicate rather than scream at age 7 so that at age 27, they are in healthy, life-giving relationships. Discipline yields its fruit over time.

This is absolutely true for the discipline of prayer as well. We should make it our aim to pray when we feel it and when we do not because every time we drag our cold hearts before the furnace of the Lord, He softens, molds, and shapes us more into His likeness. Hebrews 12:11 says, "No discipline seems enjoyable at the time, but painful. Later on, however, it yields the peaceful fruit of righteousness to those who have been trained by it." Each time we commit to pray and then keep our commitment, whether we feel it or not, we can look ahead to the fruit it will bear as we endure the discomfort of the moment.

We can also bring our lack of a desire to pray to God in prayer. Hebrews 4:16 tells us that Jesus sits on a throne of grace, that we may approach with boldness, even when we are coming begrudgingly or unimpassioned. There is forgiveness for our stubbornness and slowness to believe at His feet. Our prayer may be as simple as, "Lord, help me want to pray!"

We also have two tremendous helpers for when we do not desire to pray. The first is the Word of God. If we can not find the words to say, we can look to the Word of God and pray it back to Him. The psalms are full of prayers that can be read and prayed in times we feel at a loss for words. Psalm 51 is a great place to start.

We also have the help of the Holy Spirit, who uniquely leads and guides each believer into a deeper relationship with God by reminding us of God's Word. The Holy Spirit reminds us of the importance of prayer. When you are battling internally whether or not you will keep your commitment to pray, He may be the One who is reminding you to "Draw near to God, and he will draw near to you" (James 4:8). Ultimately, we should choose to pray even when we do not feel like it because prayer is not about us but about God. God is unchanging, eternally available, and has invited us into an intimate prayer relationship with Him.

It would make very little sense for a child to say to their parents, "Thank you for the offer to clothe, feed, and provide shelter for me, but I just do not feel like walking from the sidewalk inside the house today. I will be fine out here." Although the child may be comfortable enough for the first couple of hours, eventually, they are going to need food and a way to escape the heat and cold. Of course, they should accept the lovingly generous offer of their parents to come inside the family home.

In the same way, God has granted us access to Him in prayer through Jesus's sacrifice for our sins. When we believe in Jesus and receive God's forgiveness, we are invited into a life of prayer with God. With Him, we can commune, share our needs, receive His rest, and find continual forgiveness of sins in prayer. We may feel like rejecting this invitation if it has no effect at first, but eventually, we will end up in incredible discomfort because we simply did not feel like making an effort. Therefore, we choose to pray, not based on how we feel but on who God is.

Discipline yields its fruit over time.

daily QUESTIONS

Is it hard for you to make and keep a commitment to pray? Why or why not?

Why is it worth it to push through the discomfort of not wanting to pray? What benefits are there to prayer?

Find a psalm that you can use in your prayer time today.

LET'S pray

Let today's Bible reading and study specifically influence your prayers. Avoid reciting the same prayer every day, but bring today's praises and problems to God through this guide. As you pray today, pray the psalm you chose after you pray through the Lord's prayer.

Our Father: Write a prayer praising God for who He is. Refer to the attributes of God on pages 6-7 if needed.

_____
_____
_____
_____
_____

Your Kingdom Come: Write a prayer expressing your desire for God to build His kingdom and accomplish His will in your life and the world. Ask God to help you prioritize time to pray as that is one means through which He accomplishes His will in the world.

_____
_____
_____
_____
_____

Daily Bread: What are your physical needs today? Write a prayer asking God to do just that.

_____
_____
_____
_____
_____

Forgive Our Sins: *Take a moment to confess, and ask forgiveness for sins you have committed. As you receive God's forgiveness, remember that He has called you to forgive others.*

_____
_____
_____
_____
_____

Deliver Us: *Write a prayer asking God to help you avoid sin and stay close to Him. Ask Him to help you respond to His discipline with tenderness and humility.*

_____
_____
_____
_____
_____

> "
>
> When we believe in Jesus and receive God's forgiveness, we are invited into a life of prayer with God.

WEEK FOUR
Scripture Memory

Rejoice always,
pray constantly, give
thanks in everything;
for this is God's will for
you in Christ Jesus.

1 THESSALONIANS 5:16-18

weekly REFLECTION

Review all Scripture passages from the week.

Summarize the main points from this week's Scripture readings.

What did you observe from this week's passages about God and His character?

What do this week's passages reveal about the condition of mankind and yourself?

WEEK FOUR

How do these passages point to the gospel?

How should you respond to these Scriptures? What specific action steps can you take this week to apply them in your life?

Write a prayer in response to your study of God's Word. Adore God for who He is, confess sins He revealed in your own life, ask Him to empower you to walk in obedience, and pray for anyone who comes to mind as you study.

Lottie Diggs Moon's Story

Charlotte "Lottie" Diggs Moon was born in Albemarle County, Virginia, in 1840. In her youth, she doubted the existence of God and often rebelled against her family's religious beliefs. But, one night in her college years, desperate to deal with her confusion over God once and for all, she prayed that God would help her sort out her doubt. In the late hours of that night, God met her. And she was a devout and committed Christian from that moment forward. She knew God was real, and she could think of no better use of her life than to serve him diligently.

She attended Virginia Female Seminary and was the first single Southern Baptist woman to be appointed as a missionary to China. She fought heartily for the appointment to China as they usually did not send single women as missionaries. She sacrificially served women and children in northern China for forty years, often facing illness, depression, and at times malnutrition due to the impact of the Boxer Rebellion. She traveled more than 10,000 miles around China on her missionary journeys to share the gospel of Jesus. And even through the intense trials, she assured her friends and family that she loved and was committed to her calling of bringing the gospel to northern China.

She is quoted as having said, "As you wend your way from village to village, you feel it no idle fancy that the Master walks beside you, and you hear his voice saying gently, 'Lo, I am with you always even unto the end.'" You can almost picture her walking along a worn, rural path, praying and listening for the quiet leading of the Holy Spirit in her mission work. She lived a life steeped in continuous prayer.

In 1912, she was severely ill. Some accounts say she weighed only 50 pounds at the time. She was carried aboard a boat headed back to the United States where she could receive the medical care she desperately needed. But she never made it to the destination and died on board the boat. However, her impact has only grown in the century since her death.

She was a great advocate for inspiring women to raise funds for mission work. She often wrote letters encouraging women to support missions work in any way they could. Her advocacy led to the collection of an annual Christmas offering for mission work. The first offering in 1888 totaled $3,000, but since that time, it has raised over one billion dollars of support for mission work. Her simple, daily communion with God has impacted countless lives around the globe.

"She knew God was real, and she could think of no better use of her life than to serve him diligently."

WEEK FIVE

MAKING PRAYER

a passion

Now that we have established a practice of prayer, it is time to talk about prayer as passion. Part of establishing a healthy prayer life is simply showing up to our times of prayer and then praying. But another part of it is the awe and wonder of God whom we encounter when we pray. "Awe" and "wonder" are not apathetic words but words rooted in strong emotion.

It is possible to truly and deeply love to pray. It is possible to run to His presence with fire and fury as words eagerly spill out of your mouth to His ears. There is passion to be found in prayer. And this week we will learn how to find it!

In Christ, our salvation is eternally secure no matter what.

WEEK FIVE
day 1

The Birthplace of Passion

READ ROMANS 5:10-11, EPHESIANS 6:10-20, 2 PETER 1:3

What are you most passionate about? Your loved ones? Your health? A righteous cause? Now, can you pinpoint what makes you passionate about this thing? One could guess that your passion derives from your closeness to the object of passion.

Our loved ones are our closest relationships. The causes we champion are the ones that impact us most personally. Passion is often a result of closeness. And with prayer, it is no different. If we want to be passionate about prayer, we must first be passionate about whom we are praying to. And to be passionate about God, we must be close to Him. AW Tozer says, "To know Him is to love Him, and to know Him better is to love Him more."

How can we be close to God? Of course, there are numerous ways to be close to God. Today, we will talk about being close to God through salvation, Scripture, and steadfastness. When we learn how to be close to God and pursue closeness to Him, our passion for Him will grow. And with the growth of that passion will grow in us as well a passion for prayer.

— *Salvation* —

Before we can be close to God, we must be reconciled to God. No sinner can be in a righteous relationship with God by his own accord. God is holy and just. Since we have all sinned and fallen short of God's standards, there is no hope that we can come close to God on our own. However, Jesus lived a perfectly sinless life, meeting all of God's standards fully. And He offered His life as a ransom for all who believe. He died and accepted upon Himself the consequences for our shortcomings. This means when we believe in Jesus as Lord and that God raised Him from the dead, we are forgiven our sins and given the righteousness of Christ (Romans 5:10-11). Then, we can enter into a right relationship with

God. But that is only the beginning! Our pursuit of closeness to God does not end at that moment but continues throughout our whole earthly lives until it will be one day completed when we enter into eternity with Him in heaven.

— *Scripture* —

We pursue closeness with God when we choose to tether ourselves to His Word. The more we read the Bible, consult the Bible, meditate on the Bible, and seek to understand the Bible, the more we will know God. But we must not only know the Bible but also do what the Bible teaches. Little by little, over time, this will align our thoughts and our actions with God's desires. The more proximity we give Scripture to our lives, the more we will know God, love God, and find passion for Him.

— *Steadfastness* —

The last component to growing in closeness with God is to be steadfast. The Bible tells us over and over to stand firm in our belief in God. We see this command in 2 Corinthians 1:24, Galatians 5:1, Ephesians 6:13, Philippians 4:1, and more. In Christ, our salvation is eternally secure no matter what. But it seems if we want to continue to grow in closeness to the Lord, we should strive to stand resolutely on the truths of God we learn in Scripture. Our ability to remain steadfast depends on our trust in Scripture.

Philippians 2:13 is a great encouragement to us when we consider the strength it takes to stand strong. It says, "For it is God who is working in you both to will and to work according to his good purpose." Anything that we do for God is done because He is working within us to empower us to do it. He even gives us the desire or the "will" to do what is right. God surely equips us to stand strong!

With this in mind, there will be times when we face pressing questions about faith. In those moments, we should turn to Scripture for clarity and understanding. Scripture is sufficient. It responds to our doubts with compassion and patience. And it gives us everything we need for life and godliness (2 Peter 1:3). It may take time to find these answers. And we may feel unsure in the process. But choosing to stand firm and remain steadfast rather than to be swept away by every worry and whim is integral to remaining close to God.

And the incredible thing is that centuries of Christians can attest to this. The Bible can be tested and confronted and questioned, and it will be, time and again, confirmed as trustworthy and true. Remaining steadfast will increase your passion for God and His ways in a multitude of ways.

The first step in cultivating a passionate prayer life is to draw near to God. Passion will build as your relationship with God grows and matures. Put your life in close proximity to Him and His Word, and fight to keep it there.

God surely equips us to stand strong!

daily QUESTIONS

In which of the areas listed above (salvation, Scripture, or steadfastness) do you want to grow? How can you pursue growth in this area?

Read Ephesians 6:10-20. What do you notice about how God empowers us to stand strong? What do you notice about the ways God asks us to stand strong?

How will today's study and your evaluation of Ephesians 6:10-20 transform the way you live?

LET'S pray

Let today's Bible reading and study specifically influence your prayers. Avoid reciting the same prayer every day, but bring today's praises and problems to God through this guide.

Our Father: *Refer to the attributes of God on pages 6-7. Which of God's attributes do you want to know better? Praise Him for who He is, and ask Him to help you know Him more.*

Your Kingdom Come: *Write a prayer expressing your desire for God to build His kingdom and accomplish His will in your life and the world.*

Daily Bread: *What are your physical needs today? Write a prayer asking God to do just that.*

Forgive Our Sins: *Take a moment to confess, and ask forgiveness for sins you have committed. As you receive God's forgiveness, remember that He has called you to forgive others.*

_____
_____
_____
_____
_____

Deliver Us: *Using Philippians 2:13, write a prayer asking God to help you avoid sin and stay close to Him.*

_____
_____
_____
_____
_____
_____
_____

> We pursue closeness with God when we choose to tether ourselves to His Word.

Throughout Scripture, we see God do the miraculous in response to prayer.

WEEK FIVE

day 2

Praying for the Impossible

READ JAMES 5:13-18, 1 PETER 2:24

A disheartening diagnosis. An insurmountable financial need. A relationship that seems broken beyond repair. A seemingly unbreakable addiction. Impossible circumstances plague the world in which we live. What can we do about this? We can pray to God for whom nothing is impossible. And we should!

Throughout Scripture, we see God do the miraculous in response to prayer. The dead are raised, the sick are healed, food is provided, and demons are cast out. In James 5:13-18, we see a more robust description of praying for the impossible. If we ever pause to pray for God to intervene in miraculous ways because we think He is not able or simply does not want to, our faith will be bolstered by this passage.

James says we should pray when we suffer, when anyone is sick, and when we sin. And he says that God's response may be salvation or forgiveness, which are both kinds of spiritual healing. But God's response may also be to "raise up" or physically heal. He concludes James 5:16 by saying the prayer of a righteous person is "very powerful in its effect."

Then, in James 5:17-18, James uses the life of Elijah to illustrate the principles he taught in verses 13-16. This must mean that Elijah was a righteous person who prayed in faith and saw the effects of his prayers, right? Let us look closer at Elijah's life.

Elijah was a prophet or a spokesperson for God. God called Elijah to be a spokesperson for Him in a time when Israel was wavering in their faith and turning to pagan gods. Elijah prayed for miracles so the people would see that God was the one true God and worship Him alone in response.

In order to show the supremacy of God, Elijah prayed for drought (1 Kings 17:1-7), rain (1 Kings 18:41-46), provision of food for a widow (1 Kings 17:8-16), the raising of a boy from the dead (1 Kings 17:17-24), and more. God answered all of these prayers in miraculous form. God does indeed do miracles in response to prayers for the impossible! But does God want us to pray for miracles, too? Or were the miracles God did through Elijah only granted because God specially chose him?

The answer is that anyone who has a sincere faith in God can pray for miracles, and God will respond to these prayers according to His perfect will. Elijah was not superhuman, and the miracles God did in response to His prayers were done, not because of Elijah's greatness but for God's glory.

James says that Elijah was a human being just like we are. This means he was flawed, broken, and a sinner in need of a Savior. And this is well documented in the Bible. Elijah was fickle, fearful, and a complainer. We know he suffered from debilitating discouragement and what might be diagnosed as clinical depression today. Yet, even in his lowest moments, when he despaired of life itself, he turned to God in prayer (1 Kings 19:3-4). In one of these low moments, he feared for his life, so he ran and hid. From his hiding place, he prayed that he might die. He asked the Lord to take his life. The Lord did not grant this prayer but rather answered in a different way.

God sent an angel to feed Elijah and give him water to strengthen him for the next task the Lord called him to. Elijah regained his strength, and even though he did it with some complaining, he kept on mission after that. And what is maybe the most intriguing miracle of Elijah is that Elijah actually never died. He had prayed for God to take his life, but instead, God preserved his life in an impossible way. When Elijah's time on earth was done, God took him to heaven in a whirlwind. There is no logical explanation for this except that God chose not to let Elijah taste earthly death. A miracle! Elijah was not perfect, but He was righteous before God because of his faith (James 2:22-23).

What does this mean for us and our impossible situations? It means that if we are in Christ, we have access to bring our impossible prayer requests before God. And God has the power to do whatever it is we ask of Him. When we pray for the impossible to be done, God will not always answer by sending a miracle our way, but sometimes He will. He can do anything. We should pray for the miracles we need. He might not give us our miracles every time, but we should still ask our God, who is more than able. Where else can we go with our requests for the improbable? Nowhere. We should bring them to God.

The Lord did not grant this prayer but rather answered in a different way.

daily QUESTIONS

What did you learn about praying for the impossible through Elijah's story?

How does this inform the way you pray for the impossible?

Read Luke 1:26-38. What does this tell you about God and His ability to do the impossible?

Let today's Bible reading and study specifically influence your prayers. Avoid reciting the same prayer every day, but bring today's praises and problems to God through this guide.

Our Father: *Refer to the attributes of God on pages 6-7. Choose 2-3 and praise God for the way He embodies these in your life.*

_____
_____
_____
_____

Your Kingdom Come: *Write a prayer expressing your desire for God to build His kingdom and accomplish His will in your life and the world.*

_____
_____
_____
_____

Daily Bread: *What are your physical needs today? What impossible answers to prayer do you need today? Write a prayer asking God to meet all your needs, no matter how impossible they may seem.*

_____
_____
_____
_____

Forgive Our Sins: *Take a moment to confess, and ask forgiveness for sins you have committed. As you receive God's forgiveness, remember that He has called you to forgive others.*

_____
_____
_____
_____
_____

Deliver Us: *Using Philippians 2:13, write a prayer asking God to help you avoid sin and stay close to Him.*

_____
_____
_____
_____
_____
_____
_____

If we are in Christ, we have access to bring our impossible prayer requests before God.

Jesus carries all of His people to the Lord in prayer continuously.

WEEK FIVE

day 3

Jesus's Prayer for You

READ JOHN 17, HEBREWS 9:11-14, HEBREWS 10:20-22

John 17 contains some of the most precious words of Jesus for all Christians. In this chapter, Jesus prays a prayer for Himself, His disciples, and all believers. This prayer is referred to as the "high priestly prayer." This prayer is complex and could take a lifetime to fully understand. After all, this is a conversation between members of the Holy Trinity, so of course, it is hard to wrap our human minds around it. But what we can understand of it will ignite our souls with wonder and passion for prayer as we get a glimpse of how Jesus prays to His Father. To best understand Jesus's high priestly prayer, it will be helpful to understand some context about the role of the high priest in the Old Testament first.

When the Israelites escaped from Egypt and set up a temporary camp in the desert, they made tents for themselves to live in. They also made a tent for God's presence to reside in called the tabernacle. The tabernacle had an outer court, an inner holy place, and at its very core was the holiest place. This was where God's presence was, and it was sacred and special. Only one man was allowed to enter the most holy place—the high priest.

On the day of atonement, which happened only once a year, the high priest would enter the most holy place and offer a sacrifice and a prayer for the atonement of the sins of the entire nation. Then he would exit the most holy place, not to enter again for twelve months.

The high priest was required to wear certain attire to enter God's presence. You can read about this in Exodus 28. Their outer robe had an onyx stone on each shoulder. On these stones were inscribed the names of the twelve tribes of Israel. All Israelites belonged to one of these twelve tribes. The significance behind this was that the priest was carrying all of Israel on his shoulders into the presence of God to atone for their sins.

Jesus was the ultimate fulfillment of the role of the high priest. The earthly high priests sprinkled blood once a year, but Jesus shed his blood once for all. The earthly priests offered a prayer in God's presence one time per year. Jesus ascended to the right hand of God after He sacrificed His life and has not ceased praying for His people ever since. He sits permanently in the presence of God and prays for all believers, even today. The Old Testament high priest carried the Israelites on his shoulders when He entered the most holy place. Jesus carries all of His people to the Lord in prayer continuously.

This prayer in John 17 shows us the type of intercessory prayers Jesus prayed when He brought His people to the Father in prayer. His prayers for His disciples are that God would protect the disciples in His name, that the disciples may be one even as He and the Father were one, and that His joy would be complete in the disciples. He went on to pray that God would keep the disciples from the evil one and that God would sanctify the disciples in truth.

Jesus prays that all believers would be one as the Father is in the Son and the Son is in the Father, that all believers would be in the Father and the Son so the world may know that the Father sent the Son, and that all believers would be with Him where He is and see His glory. He concludes by praying that the love with which the Father loved the Son would be in all believers and that He would be in all believers.

What a precious gift it is to see Jesus's prayers for those who believe spelled out so plainly for us. If you are a Christian, Jesus desires for you all the things listed above! And even now, He is interceding for you at the right hand of God (Hebrews 7:24-25). We have spent this study learning about prayer from many different aspects, and this may be the most important one: prayer is not just something you do but something Jesus Himself does for you!

> *The earthly high priests sprinkled blood once a year, but Jesus shed his blood once for all.*

daily QUESTIONS

Read John 17:6-26. What does Jesus's high priestly prayer teach you about Him?

What does Jesus's high priestly prayer teach you about yourself?

How do the truths you listed in questions 1 and 2 impact your prayer life?

LET'S pray

Let today's Bible reading and study specifically influence your prayers. Avoid reciting the same prayer every day, but bring today's praises and problems to God through this guide.

Our Father: *Refer to your answer to question 1. Write a prayer praising Jesus for who He is.*

_____
_____
_____
_____
_____

Your Kingdom Come: *According to the high priestly prayer in John 17, what does God want to do in your life and in the world? Write a prayer expressing your desire for God to build His kingdom in these ways.*

_____
_____
_____
_____
_____

Daily Bread: *What are your physical needs today? Write a prayer asking God to meet all your needs.*

_____
_____
_____
_____
_____

Forgive Our Sins: *Take a moment to confess, and ask forgiveness for sins you have committed. As you receive God's forgiveness, remember that He has called you to forgive others.*

_____
_____
_____
_____
_____

Deliver Us: *Using Philippians 2:13, write a prayer asking God to help you avoid sin and stay close to Him.*

_____
_____
_____
_____
_____
_____
_____

Prayer is not just something you do but something Jesus Himself does for you!

Persistent prayer is a part of every believer's life.

WEEK FIVE

day 4

Persistent Prayer

READ LUKE 18:1-8, LUKE 11:5-13, 2 PETER 3:8-9

Making prayer a habit is much more than simply adding it to your daily calendar. Prayer requires not just some effort but a profound effort. It requires persistence. Therefore, part of making prayer a habit is learning to be long-suffering and tenacious in prayer.

A stick-shift car has several gears that allow it to travel at different speeds without putting too much strain on the engine. A lower gear only allows the car to travel at slow speeds without overworking the engine, snapping the valves, and damaging the transmission. When it is time to switch gears, the rotations per minute of the pistons will reach what is called the redline zone. Manual car drivers must constantly watch for their RPMs to enter the redline zone and shift accordingly to more comfortably drive at a higher speed. Similarly, there are times when practicing prayer means switching gears mentally and spiritually.

We all hope that God will answer our prayers immediately, but often this is not the case. In these moments, instead of quitting prayer out of frustration, anger, or bitterness, imagine that the friction you are experiencing is like a manual shift car, revving into the redline zone. It is time to adjust gears in your prayer life. You must shift from praying for an immediate answer to praying with persistence for an answer. It is a totally different gear. It still requires constant and fervent prayer. It does not mean you stop praying but rather that you have committed to continue praying for as long as it takes.

Persistent prayer is mentioned in Luke 18:1-8. It is a fascinating parable told by Jesus about a poor, lowly widow who was seeking justice from an adversary by bringing her case before a judge. The judge was unrighteous and did not fear God or man. He snubbed the widow repeatedly. But the widow, in her distress, did not give up. It was not because he was kind but because she was persistent that he eventually heard her case and relieved her from her adversary.

Jesus tells this story then says, "Will not God grant justice to his elect who cry out to him day and night?" (Luke 18:7). He is showing that God is unlike the unrighteous judge. If a judge with no regard for people will do such a thing, then how much more will God, who cares specifically for each of His children, hear their prayers and carefully answer? Infinitely more.

Jesus goes on to explain that God gives justice speedily, not by our standards but by His. God does not delay, but He does show patience toward all, not willing that any should perish (2 Peter 3:8-9). The justice Jesus mentions might be earthly and momentary justice. God does give that freely. But it will be ultimately fulfilled in the throne of justice and peace Jesus will establish upon His return. And until then, we live in a world where it is only partially fulfilled.

Until the moment that Jesus returns and rights all wrongs and corrects every injustice, He asks that we always pray and do not lose heart. He asks us to pray with persistence. God's redemptive plan for the earth is in motion. We are perfectly and enduringly hurtling toward eternal peace. We must believe this. And we must be okay with shifting gears from immediately to persistently, clinging to Jesus Himself who says to us that we must not lose heart in the time it takes for prayers to be answered.

We pray not to an unrighteous judge but a tender Father. We can run to him over and over and over again. And we will need to. Persistent prayer is a part of every believer's life. Prayer cannot be practiced biblically without it.

Jesus ends this parable with the perfect question for us to consider today. He asks, "when the Son of Man comes, will he find faith on earth?" Will He find those still persistently watching, waiting, and praying for His just answer? Will you continue to pray in faith and with endurance? Is it time for you to shift gears and settle in for the long haul with persistent prayer?

"

God's redemptive plan for the earth is in motion.

daily QUESTIONS

Do you pray with persistence? Is it easy or hard for you?

Is there a prayer request that you need to "switch gears" from immediate to persistent prayer?

How can you cling to Jesus and not lose heart while you persistently pray?

LET'S pray

Let today's Bible reading and study specifically influence your prayers. Avoid reciting the same prayer every day, but bring today's praises and problems to God through this guide.

Our Father: What do we learn about who God is through the story of the persistent widow in Luke 18:1-8? Based on this, write a prayer praising God for who He is.

_____
_____
_____
_____

Your Kingdom Come: Write a prayer expressing your desire for God to build His kingdom and accomplish His will in and around you.

_____
_____
_____
_____

Daily Bread: What are your physical needs today? Maybe you need God to grant you the perseverance to continue to pray for a need that you have had for a long time. Write a prayer asking God to meet all your needs.

_____
_____
_____
_____

Forgive Our Sins: *Take a moment to confess, and ask forgiveness for sins you have committed. As you receive God's forgiveness, remember that He has called you to forgive others.*

_____
_____
_____
_____
_____

Deliver Us: *Write a prayer asking God to help you avoid sin and stay close to Him.*

_____
_____
_____
_____
_____
_____
_____

> **"**
>
> We pray not to an unrighteous judge but a tender Father. We can run to him over and over and over again.

Because His return is not far off and not delayed, we should live in anticipation of it.

WEEK FIVE

day 5

Scripture's Final Prayer

READ REVELATION 21:1-5, REVELATION 22:13-21, 1 CORINTHIANS 16:22, ACTS 1:6-7

There is no more fitting end to our study of prayer than to look at the final prayer in the Bible. We find it in the last chapter of the last book of the Bible, which is called Revelation. Revelation is a fascinating and sometimes confusing book and is classified as apocalyptic literature. What is apocalyptic literature? Believe it or not, it is not writing about the end of the world. "Apocalypse" comes from a Greek word that means "to uncover or reveal." Apocalyptic literature in the Bible reveals the world as it actually is. It gives a glimpse into the spiritual reality of the world.

Throughout Revelation, you will see war, famine, and a battle between Jesus and evil portrayed in vivid images. These images show the spiritual realities at play in the world behind the physical realities we see and experience. Much of the book outlines how evil forces (a beast, a dragon, and a woman) bring chaos and death to mankind while Jesus (the slain lamb) protects and defends His people. The scene is often grim and bloody. And while it can be hard to read, no one could ignore the fact that we do see evil, just as described in this book, playing out in the world around us.

Though the whole earth is groaning under the weight of evil for the first twenty chapters of Revelation, there is a triumphant victory at the end of the book! Jesus defeats Satan. Satan and his whole cast of deceivers and demons are thrown into a lake of fire from which they can never escape. The earth is now permanently free from these evil influences, and a new kind of kingdom is established on earth. This kingdom looks just like heaven. Does this sound familiar? It is "on earth as it is in heaven."

God comes down and dwells with man again on earth. Revelation 21:4 describes it like this, "He will wipe away every tear from their eyes. Death will be no more; grief, crying, and pain will be no more, because the previous things have passed away."

All of the anguish, despair, injustices, and horrors that once plagued the earth are gone. And in their place is being established a new heaven and earth where King Jesus reigns forevermore. When this takes place, those who believe in Jesus and are saved will take part in the glorious new earth with Him. Oh, what joy! Oh, what peace! Oh, what rest! Oh, how we long for that day.

But we do not know when that day will come. Acts 1:6-7 says that we do not know the day or the hour of Christ's return. Even Christ Himself does not know it, but only the Father. But what we do know is that He is coming soon. And because His return is not far off and not delayed, we should live in anticipation of it. One way we do this is to pray earnestly that He would come.

Revelation 22:20 says, "He who testifies about these things says, 'Yes, I am coming soon.' Amen! Come, Lord Jesus!" The first part of this verse contains the words of Jesus affirming that His coming is not a long way off but soon. And the second part of this verse is what John, the author of Revelation, uttered in response to this glorious truth. "Amen! Come, Lord Jesus!"

In that short four-word prayer is wrapped all the hope of humanity. Jesus came once and made a way for all mankind to come into a loving relationship with the Father. Yet, we still experience the brutal effects of sin. But when Jesus comes again, He will defeat sin and death completely. It is to this truth that we cling. And it is with this prayer that we join our voice with all of creation in crying for the final redemption and restoration that is to come.

There is no other way we could end our study of prayer than by praying together, *Come, Lord Jesus! Come and take Your place as King. We wait for You with bated breath. You are our only hope now and forevermore.*

"

When Jesus comes again, He will defeat sin and death completely.

daily QUESTIONS

Read Revelation 21. Describe the new heaven and new earth that Jesus will establish after His second coming and the defeat of sin and death.

Read Revelation 22, and highlight every time Jesus says He is coming soon. Why do you think He repeated this phrase so many times in the final chapter of the Bible?

How does an understanding of the second coming of Christ transform how you live today?

Let today's Bible reading and study specifically influence your prayers. Avoid reciting the same prayer every day, but bring today's praises and problems to God through this guide.

Our Father: What attributes of God did you see on display in Revelation 21-22? Refer to the attributes of God on pages 6-7 if needed. Write a prayer praising God for embodying these qualities.

_____
_____
_____
_____

Your Kingdom Come: Write a prayer expressing your desire for Jesus to return and redeem the whole earth so that it is "on earth as it is in heaven."

_____
_____
_____
_____
_____

Daily Bread: What are your physical needs today? Write a prayer asking God to meet all your needs. Include a prayer of thanksgiving for how all your needs will be met when the earth is redeemed after the second coming of Christ.

_____
_____
_____
_____
_____
_____

Forgive Our Sins: *Take a moment to confess, and ask forgiveness for sins you have committed. As you receive God's forgiveness, remember that He has called you to forgive others.*

Deliver Us: *Write a prayer asking God to help you avoid sin and stay close to Him.*

"

"Amen! Come, Lord Jesus!"
In that short four-word prayer is wrapped
all the hope of humanity.

WEEK FIVE

Scripture Memory

———————————————————

He who testifies about these
things says, "Yes, I am coming
soon." Amen! Come, Lord Jesus!

REVELATION 22:20

weekly REFLECTION

Review all Scripture passages from the week.

Summarize the main points from this week's Scripture readings.

What did you observe from this week's passages about God and His character?

What do this week's passages reveal about the condition of mankind and yourself?

WEEK FIVE

How do these passages point to the gospel?

How should you respond to these Scriptures? What specific action steps can you take this week to apply them in your life?

Write a prayer in response to your study of God's Word. Adore God for who He is, confess sins He revealed in your own life, ask Him to empower you to walk in obedience, and pray for anyone who comes to mind as you study.

Martin Luther's Prayer

Behold, Lord,
An empty vessel that needs to be filled.
My Lord, fill it.
I am weak in faith;
Strengthen thou me.
I am cold in love;
Warm me and make me fervent
That my love may go out to my neighbour.
I do not have a strong and firm faith;
At times I doubt and am unable to trust thee altogether.
O Lord, help me.
Strengthen my faith and trust in thee.
In thee I have sealed the treasures of all I have.
I am poor;
Thou art rich and didst come to be merciful to the poor.
I am a sinner;
Thou art upright.
With me there is an abundance of sin;
In thee is the fullness of righteousness.
Therefore, I will remain with thee of who I can receive
But to whom I may not give.
Amen.

What's Next?

Congrats! You have finished this five-week study on prayer!

Our hope is that you have established a passionate practice of prayer in your daily life. But, truly, this study is just the beginning. You have a lifetime of prayer ahead of you!

Consider checking out some of the other great resources on prayer from The Daily Grace Co. to help you continue to grow in prayer.

We have even included a sample of the *In Everything Prayer Journal* on pages 208-209.

Additional resources for prayer

Abide Journal

The Abide Journal is an all-in-one prayer and Bible study journal. It features tabs for Bible Study, Prayer, Weekly Reflection of gratitude and Adoration. It also includes a notes section that can be used for sermon notes, quotes, or anything else.

Prayers for Your Day

Prayers for Your Day is a booklet filled with prayers for every part of the day as well as for various seasons of life, different emotions, marriage, children, and even new friendships.

In Everything Prayer Journal

The *In Everything Journal* is one of our favorite tools ever! This journal is customizable and practical. It is designed to help you pray intentionally, with space for your prayer requests, Scripture to pray, and space to write down what God is teaching you.

31 Days of Prayer Verse Card Set

This is a set of 31 verse cards. Each card includes Scripture to pray and several prompts to guide you in prayer. Cards include prompts to pray for friends, neighbors, wisdom, contentment, unbelievers, persecuted Christians, and more.

DATE   /   /   REQUEST FOR:

_____
_____
_____

SCRIPTURE TO PRAY: _____
_____
_____

———————— GOD IS TEACHING ME ————————

ANSWERED ON   /   /
_____
_____

DATE   /   /   REQUEST FOR:

_____
_____
_____

SCRIPTURE TO PRAY: _____
_____
_____

———————— GOD IS TEACHING ME ————————

ANSWERED ON   /   /
_____
_____

DATE / /   REQUEST FOR:

_____
_____
_____

SCRIPTURE TO PRAY: _____
_____
_____

──── GOD IS TEACHING ME ────

ANSWERED ON / /

_____
_____

DATE / /   REQUEST FOR:

_____
_____
_____

SCRIPTURE TO PRAY: _____
_____
_____

──── GOD IS TEACHING ME ────

ANSWERED ON / /

_____
_____

What is the Gospel?

THANK YOU FOR READING AND ENJOYING THIS STUDY WITH US! WE ARE ABUNDANTLY GRATEFUL FOR THE WORD OF GOD, THE INSTRUCTION WE GLEAN FROM IT, AND THE EVER-GROWING UNDERSTANDING IT PROVIDES FOR US OF GOD'S CHARACTER. WE ARE ALSO THANKFUL THAT SCRIPTURE CONTINUALLY POINTS TO ONE THING IN INNUMERABLE WAYS: THE GOSPEL.

We remember our brokenness when we read about the fall of Adam and Eve in the garden of Eden (Genesis 3), where sin entered into a perfect world and maimed it. We remember the necessity that something innocent must die to pay for our sin when we read about the atoning sacrifices in the Old Testament. We read that we have all sinned and fallen short of the glory of God (Romans 3:23) and that the penalty for our brokenness, the wages of our sin, is death (Romans 6:23). We all need grace and mercy, but most importantly, we all need a Savior.

We consider the goodness of God when we realize that He did not plan to leave us in this dire state. We see His promise to buy us back from the clutches of sin and death in Genesis 3:15. And we see that promise accomplished with Jesus Christ on the cross. Jesus Christ knew no sin yet became sin so that we might become righteous through His sacrifice (2 Corinthians 5:21). Jesus was tempted in every way that we are and lived sinlessly. He was reviled yet still yielded Himself for our sake, that we may have life abundant in Him. Jesus lived the perfect life that we could not live and died the death that we deserved.

The gospel is profound yet simple. There are many mysteries in it that we will never understand this side of heaven, but there is still overwhelming weight to its implications in this life. The gospel tells of our sinfulness and God's goodness and a gracious gift that compels a response. We are saved by grace through faith, which means that we rest with faith in the grace that Jesus Christ displayed on the cross (Ephesians 2:8-9). We cannot save ourselves from our brokenness or do any amount of good works to merit God's favor. Still, we can have faith that what Jesus accomplished in His death, burial, and resurrection was more than enough for our salvation and our eternal delight. When we accept God, we are commanded to die to ourselves and our sinful desires and live a life worthy of the calling we have received (Ephesians 4:1). The gospel compels us to be sanctified, and in so doing, we are conformed to the likeness of Christ Himself. This is hope. This is redemption. This is the gospel.

SCRIPTURES TO REFERENCE:

GENESIS 3:15	*I will put hostility between you and the woman, and between your offspring and her offspring. He will strike your head, and you will strike his heel.*
ROMANS 3:23	*For all have sinned and fall short of the glory of God.*
ROMANS 6:23	*For the wages of sin is death, but the gift of God is eternal life in Christ Jesus our Lord.*
2 CORINTHIANS 5:21	*He made the one who did not know sin to be sin for us, so that in him we might become the righteousness of God.*
EPHESIANS 2:8-9	*For you are saved by grace through faith, and this is not from yourselves; it is God's gift—not from works, so that no one can boast.*
EPHESIANS 4:1-3	*Therefore I, the prisoner in the Lord, urge you to walk worthy of the calling you have received, with all humility and gentleness, with patience, bearing with one another in love, making every effort to keep the unity of the Spirit through the bond of peace.*

*Thank you for studying
God's Word with us!*

CONNECT WITH US
@thedailygraceco
@dailygracepodcast

CONTACT US
info@thedailygraceco.com

SHARE
#thedailygraceco

VISIT US ONLINE
www.thedailygraceco.com

MORE DAILY GRACE
The Daily Grace App
Daily Grace Podcast